GW00503592

# Angling Boats

# A Guide To Owning And Running A Small Boat For Sea Angling

## Neville Merritt

**ARFORD BOOKS**

BORDON • HAMPSHIRE

## Angling Boats

A Guide To
Owning And
Running
A Small
Boat For
Sea Angling

First published in 2006 by
ARFORD BOOKS
Apple Tree, Arford Road, Headley
Bordon, Hampshire GU35 8BT
Tel: 01428 713019

ISBN 10 : 0-9553242-0-3
ISBN 13 : 978-0-9553242-0-8

Produced and printed by
members of
THE GUILD OF MASTER
CRAFTSMEN

**Cover Design and text illustrations:**
Ian Tyrrell
**Text Diagrams:**
Neville Merritt
**Book Design and Typesetting:**
Cecil Smith
Typeset in Giovanni Book and
Poppl-Laudatio

Printed and bound in Great Britain
by
RPM PRINT & DESIGN
2-3 Spur Road, Quarry Lane,
Chichester, West Sussex PO19 8PR

# Acknowledgements

I started writing this book feeling slightly fraudulent, as I am no expert at the subject – after boating for over thirty years, I am still learning a lot. What I have written has been learned from the many people who have helped me over the years, plus a little from my own trial and error. So the least I can do is to acknowledge who has taught me.

I would like to thank the writers of the many books and boating articles I have read; those that patiently taught me on boating, navigation and VHF courses; the many acquaintances at the waterside who freely gave advice to a complete stranger; my friends on various web angling forums and my father who passed on to me his love of the sea. And above all, I would like to thank my wife and children, who let me disappear whenever the tides and wind are right…

# Contents

# Introduction

I decided to write this book because I came across many questions on web forums asking for help on the basics of owning a boat. I realised that I had asked the same questions once, and it took years to find all the answers. There are many people willing to help, and there are countless books and magazines, but I have never come across a book as an introduction to boats written with anglers in mind. This is it.

The sea is a resource we must all be able to share. Angling is not the only water sport – there are yachts, dinghies, powerboats, jet-skis, windsurfers and more. Other boaters may not understand what we, as anglers, do – nor do all anglers understand the intricacies of other water sports. So please be tolerant of other boats and leave room for others to enjoy the water, and hope they do the same for you.

As a knowledgeable boat owner, you will be part of the community that shares a deep respect for the sea, and you will find a tremendous camaraderie among boat owners. Any of us may need help at any time, and it is more common for someone to go out of their way to help than pass on by.

This book was written as a "get you started" guide, so it provides the basic information you need to have on a range of topics. Many specialist books have been written on each area covered. Once you have a general grasp of what to do with your boat, and if you want to explore areas such as navigation, there are plenty more sources on the web, in magazines, books, videos and courses. I hope you will want to find out more.

Above all, have fun and be safe. Happy boating and tight lines.

*Neville Merritt*
*2006*

# Why Buy a Boat

You will hear these sooner or later:

*"A boat is a hole in the water into which
you pour money"*

*"Owning a boat is like standing in a cold shower
tearing up ten pound notes"*

Joking apart, why do you want to own a boat? It would be a good idea to be sure you know why you are doing it, because believe me, it is going to cost a lot of time and money. This is not an attempt to put you off, but plenty of boat salesmen have earned good commissions on boats used just a few times before they are sold on.

So let's have a look at a few reasons to buy a small fishing boat, and perhaps dispel a few myths before it is too late.

1.  **I would save on charter boat fees.** Wrong. Have a look at the annual costs of running a boat, divide by the number of outings you usually have and I think you'll see that running your own boat is no bargain. There are compensations, or nobody would do it, but don't believe it is a cheap option.

2.  **I can fish more often.** This depends. If you leave you boat in the water and you can easily fit in some short trips, you may well get more fishing in. But running a fishing boat takes time, and chances are your spare time will be taken up by maintenance and general fiddling. Also, there is more to a fishing trip by boat than jumping in and driving off. You have to prepare for each trip, and clean up and tidy down afterwards. If you have to trail your boat and launch every time, then you need to include the launch and recovery times as well. It all adds up!

3.  **I like boat fishing, so owning a boat seems logical.** As I mentioned before, there is a lot more to running a boat than fishing from it. Try turning that statement around and it would make more sense – "I like boats so fishing from it seems logical".

The message is – make sure you like boating! You will have to put a lot of time, money and effort into running your own boat safely and reliably, so there has to be an incentive. If you have, or develop an interest in boats, then there is no problem – it will be a labour of love. You won't mind going down to the marina in a howling gale just to make sure everything is OK. You won't mind scraping off the antifouling in April while your mates are out after the plaice. And you won't mind taking the family for a spin round the harbour when you are sure the bass are under those terns diving over the sand-bar. You won't mind because you enjoy boats as much as fishing.

Having established that you really do want to run a boat of your own, it would be wise to have a look at all the costs involved before you stump up the money for the boat itself. Obviously I don't know how large a boat you are thinking of, or what the costs are in your part of the world, so I cannot list the actual costs. What I will do however is provide a checklist of the items and services that you will have to invest in both up front and on an ongoing basis. Use this checklist to cost up various options before you start – and add a bit more for contingencies. It would be a huge disappointment if you invested in a boat then realised you could not meet all the other costs involved. And don't think you can sell a boat just like a car – it often takes months for a second-hand boat to find a buyer, particularly out of season.

| Items | Cost |
|---|---|
| Boat Purchase cost | |
| Trailer and lock | |
| Engine | |
| Spare engine | |
| Navigation and Electronics if not already fitted: Compass Fishfinder VHF Radio and aerial GPS Charts | |
| Anchor and rope | |
| Flares | |
| Lifejackets | |
| Second fuel tank and battery | |
| Fenders and mooring ropes | |
| Other bits: buckets, pump if not already fitted, seats, rod holders etc. | |
| **Total** | |
| Annual Costs: Annual Engine Service Trailer brakes and bearing service Storage or marina fees Insurance VHF Radio Licence Replace flares every 3 years | |
| **Total** | |

**Semi
Displacement
Hull**

**Deep Vee
High Speed Hull**

**Catamaran
Hull**

# Boats To Choose From

There are hundreds of different types of boat, to suit different uses, lifestyles and pockets. You can of course fish from any boat as long as it is in the right spot, but some boats are more suitable as a dedicated fishing platform than others. In this section we will ignore all the boats not intended primarily for fishing and concentrate on the different hull, layout and engine choices to choose from. If you intend to fish from a boat that will have other uses, such as a family power boat or sailing cruiser, then you need to choose a boat to suit all uses – but there are horses for courses and your family sailing cruiser may not be the best boat for a wrecking trip!

**RIB**

**Centre Console Dory**

The size of a boat is usually referred to by length, until you get to large commercial vessels where they are referred to by tonnage. The smallest boat you can reasonably fish from is about four metres in length, and you would need to keep within a couple of miles of the shore. At five metres you can start to get more adventurous, and friends of mine with seven and eight metre boats are regularly going to wrecks thirty miles off shore and more. But size comes with a price. A seven metre boat is not just a bit more than a six metre boat – it can be more than 50% more expensive because as length increases, so does width, depth, thickness of hull, fittings and so on. So size is one decision you will have to make, and that will in turn determine where it is practical to keep it. Up to six metres is launchable from a good slipway, so you could keep it ashore. Above that length you will have to consider marina fees or moorings and keep the boat in the water. Also, length of boat usually determines the marina or mooring fees which are calculated by boat length per year. We will cover storage later on.

# Types of Boat

Having decided on an approximate length of boat you will now be faced with an array of choices of hull shape and internal layout. Let's look at the hull shape first. This starts simply then gets a bit more complex. Basically there are two families of hull – slow and fast. The slow hulls are hull shapes that sit "in" the water and the engine pushes the boat through it. Fast boats have planing hulls which are designed to rise up and skim along the surface at speed, and these come in a variety of styles. The following are the general hull shapes you will come across.

## Displacement

The traditional boat shape that has been unchanged for hundreds of years is referred to as displacement – named because it displaces water as it pushes through it. This is an excellent hull for low speed, economical use with good sea-keeping qualities and a stable platform at anchor. The only problem is that there will always be an upper limit of speed – which is proportional to the length of the hull, but we won't go into that here. If you want to spend as little as possible on boat and engine, this is the hull for you, but don't expect to get anywhere fast. A small displacement fishing boat will reach around 10 knots at the most, which means it will take you a lot longer to reach your fishing grounds than a planing boat – but you will use much less fuel and you will have a pleasant ride. Thousands of displacement boats are available, and have only become less popular recently because people want to get out to the fishing grounds fast – which in some over-fished areas is becoming further and further offshore.

**Semi Displacement Hull**

## Semi Displacement

This is a development of the displacement hull where some clever naval architects have designed a hull shape like a traditional boat which behaves like a true displacement hull at low speed, but with sufficient engine power can be persuaded to plane, giving higher cruising and top speeds but not as high as the true planing hulls. It is a good compromise for the traditionalist who wants a bit more top speed, and can cope well with heavy weather.

## Shallow Vee

This refers to the slab-sided, almost flat bottomed hull you will find on most boats designed for inland use on rivers and canals, although in fact it was the first high speed hull design. They allow for plenty of room inside, but are top-heavy and can be downright dangerous in anything but a gentle wave. These hulls are not recommended for sea fishing boats unless you are confining your adventures to estuaries, harbours and very calm days.

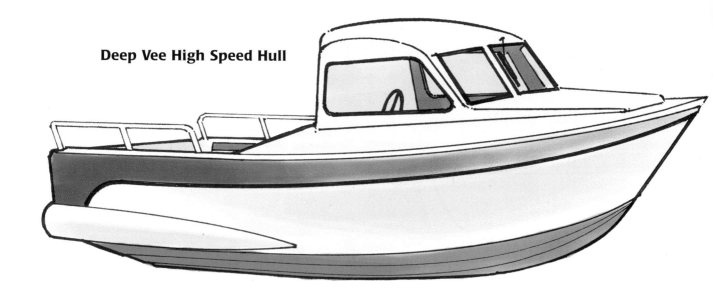

**Deep Vee High Speed Hull**

## Deep Vee

This is a common style of high speed hull and if you look under a typical speedboat you will see what I mean. The hull, conceived by Ray Hunt in 1963, is designed to slide over rather than through the water which reduces the water resistance and allows higher speeds to be reached. When you first start off there is a lot of fuss and bother as the engines strain to push the boat "onto the plane", but once there (at around ten knots in my seven metre Trophy) you quickly pick up speed and fly off. Planing hulls can be designed to reach very high speeds on expensive powerboats but typically on a fishing boat you can expect to find ones that cruise at 20 to 25 knots with top speeds of 30 to 40 knots.

That speed comes at a price – as the engines needed to push the hull onto the plane and maintain those high speeds are not likely to be small, and big engines drink fuel. The other disadvantage is in the ride comfort. On a smooth sea, the high speed runs can be exhilarating, but in a short choppy sea where the boat is constantly crashing into waves that can be very uncomfortable indeed. A lot depends on weight, and boat length ratio to wave length, but believe me, pushing a light eighteen foot planing hull into a fresh breeze will shake your fillings out. Larger, heavier boats will still crash around a bit but their weight will tend to smooth the bumps and you will find the ride more comfortable. In heavier weather however, you will not be able to plane and your speed will be severely restricted, unlike the displacement hulls which just keep on going. This is worth considering when the wind is rising, you have a 20 mile trip home and you need to cross the sandbar at the harbour entrance by dusk!

## Cathedral Hull

Also referred to as "dory" hulls, this shape looks like a cross between a boat and a catamaran, as the front half of the hull becomes two mini planning hulls. This has the advantage of keeping the boat shape fairly square, increasing the internal useable space without losing out on performance. You usually find these hulls only on boats less than twenty feet long, and they can slam a bit in choppy seas. However there is a good choice of small boats with these hulls which make roomy fishing platforms with a good turn of speed. The downside? They are just plain ugly and look like mobile baths, but that is just a personal opinion.

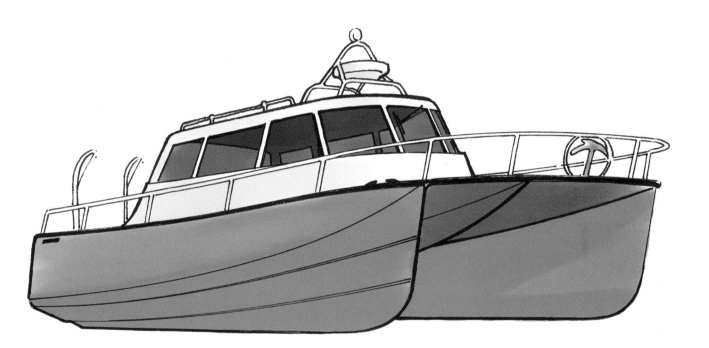

**Catamaran Hull**

## Catamaran

Originally catamaran hulls were confined to yachts where two narrow hulls allowed for greater speed and stability. There are now some catamaran or "cat" hulls for fishing boats, that take the form of two planing hulls joined together to form a wide, stable platform. They are usually only available for larger boats of eight metres and above, as the working deck space has to sit above the hulls rather than in them, but they have enormous fishing space and can be quite fast. The downside is the ugliness again ,and also that marinas usually charge extra because of the sideways space they take up.

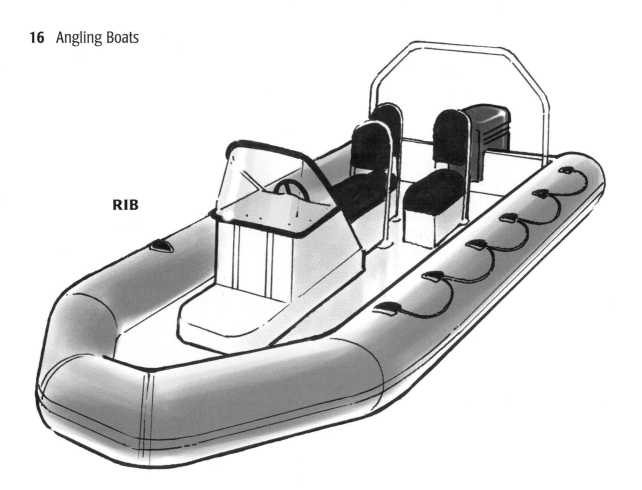

**RIB**

## Rigid Inflatables or RIBs

Much favoured by divers, RIBs are made with a bottom of a rigid planing hull surrounded by an inflatable tube, which makes then fast, low enough to get in and out of – and very wet. They are easy to launch and manoeuvre, but the lack of a "side" which makes them excellent dive boats does not help much for fishing boats. I would also worry about the many sharp items of fishing equipment damaging the inflatable membrane, but if you are after a multi-purpose boat it could be worth considering. I know a number of keen bass angles fish from RIBs right under the cliffs on the South Coast, as they can get in where conventional boats would have a problem.

## Engines

Like hulls, this is worth a book by itself so I will keep it very simple and point out the choices. There are three main fuel types: petrol, in two- or four-stroke versions, and diesel. Petrol has two very important disadvantages – you pay road tax on all petrol even for marine use so it is currently more than twice the price of "red" diesel available for non-road users; and it is explosive. Many fire-related marine disasters have had something to do with petrol igniting, so you have to be very careful. At sea you are a long way away from the fire service!

So why would you bother with petrol? Fortunately there are compensations – petrol engines are much lighter and cheaper so if your fuel consumption will not be very high, the purchase price plus running costs for petrol may well be cheaper than the diesel option. However you need to balance that with the higher complexity of a petrol engine with its dependence on electrics, which has more things to go wrong. Being lighter they are also less ruggedly built and tend to have a shorter life. If money was no object most people would go for diesel, and when you come to sell your petrol-engined boat on the second-hand market you will see what I mean. There are some LPG conversions available for petrol, but like road users there are relatively few filling points and you have all the disadvantages of the petrol engine apart from the fuel costs.

There are three main categories of engine style. First and most commonly used in smaller boats is the outboard, many are two-stroke but four stroke petrol models are becoming a lot more common. They are light, relatively cheap and easy to get at for installation and maintenance. They are also easy to steal and that is the biggest liability – even engines bolted to the transom have been cut out with chainsaws and never seen again.

Inboard engines are mounted inboard, obviously, and drive the boat via a propeller shaft and external propeller. Having the engine inboard towards the centre of the boat helps to centralise and stabilise the weight distribution and means that if anything goes wrong at sea the engine is a lot easier to get at than an outboard hanging off the stern. The only real disadvantage of an inboard set-up is the fact that the propeller is fixed in a fairly inaccessible part of the boat – right underneath, which will be the first part to bang a rock if you misjudge the depth, and if you pick up a plastic bag around it, it will usually involve a swim to clear it. The propeller is highly vulnerable when launching from a slipway so if you plan to trail your boat, then an inboard set-up may not be the best. Inboard powered boats are steered with a rudder, unlike either the outboard or the final style we will look at; the out-drive.

The out-drive is a cross between the first two. The engine is often the same as the inboard, but mounted right next to the stern and fixed directly to an out-drive leg, which is like the bottom half of an outboard motor but contains only the gearbox, steering and propeller. Like an outboard, it can be lifted up when the need arises but is rather vulnerable to the elements as it is a complex piece of machinery, left in the water for months on end. It is mainly used for fast hulls and suits some boat layouts very well as the engine casing is out of the way against the stern making more room in the centre of the boat.

The final question on engines is – how many. Two is better than one from a safety point of view, and there are many twin outboard, out-drive and inboard boats around. But two engines means higher costs – both to buy and to maintain, and with the increased reliability of modern engines, having two is not as essential as it once was. Many angling boats have a smaller outboard as a backup engine but there are considerations. You have to take account of where you would keep it when it is not being used, you would need a fairly large auxiliary engine to get you home if there was a problem, and being petrol driven, you are back with the old petrol problems again. In addition, a petrol-engined outboard that is rarely used is not a device I would like to rely on in an emergency. However, it is better to have some form of reserve power than nothing at all, particularly if your main engine is a petrol-powered outboard.

## Internal Layout

If this was a book about family cruisers this would be a long section. As it is a book for anglers, I will keep it to the essentials – you can have a look at all the options on the market for yourself. I will briefly explain the different types of internal layout, give you a few questions to think about and leave it at that.

If you want no-frills boating, go for an open boat. This is basically a hull, an engine and nothing else. This style is usually only for displacement boats under six metres but remember, if you want any protection you'll have to wear it.

Going up a notch you can go for a boat with some basic protection. A small cabin, with either an open back or a bulkhead is usually called a cuddy if there are no berths or other facilities in it, and for smaller boats this will provide useful weather protection and storage for little extra weight or expense. There is another style of protection much used in warmer climates and now appearing in Europe and that is the centre console style. This is common on fast open boats up to around seven metres long, and is a control platform with steering, instruments and a windscreen, with something for the helmsman to perch on. This is a more comfortable arrangement for a fast boat if you want access all around. This is also the usual layout for RIBs and dories.

You may also come across the term "Walkaround" style, usually associated with boats built in the USA. These are mainly designed for water sports where access to deck space is more important than cabin space. These designs make excellent angling platforms, with wide, safe side decks which are gained at the minor expense of slightly narrower helm positions or cabin. Most models have open tops with a hard sun shelter as an option. Some have cuddy options for the Canadian market, which are more suited to our European weather conditions.

**Centre Console Dory**

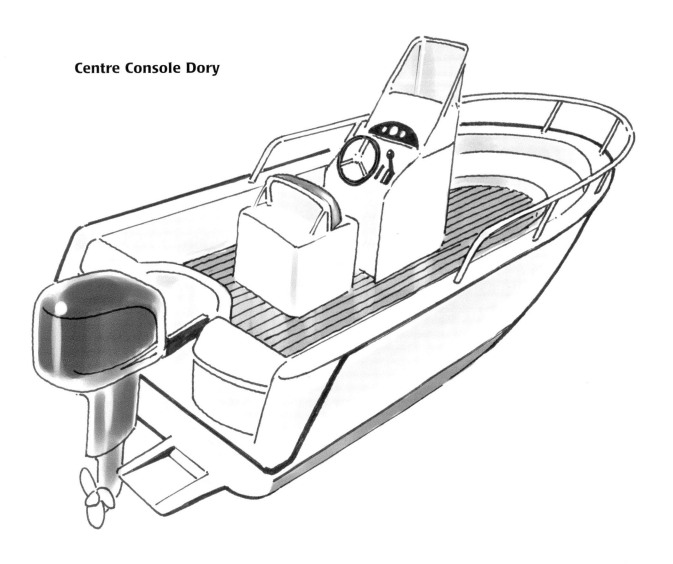

The next step up is to have a cabin, and then perhaps a cabin with a separate wheelhouse. The more cabin you have, the less fishing space you will be left with, but on a long trip where you might want to brew up, change into dry clothes, go to the toilet without an audience, get out of the cold wind or even sleep, a wheelhouse and cabin can be great. Cabins can be basic affairs or very luxurious, and it is amazing what miracles can be worked on tiny spaces, and we have the huge cruiser market to thank for that. The French have a category of boat called a Promenade-a-Peche, which is a comfortable mini cruiser designed for the angler to fish from, and very nice they are too.

## Boatbuilding Materials

I expect almost all the boats you will be looking at will be fibreglass (also referred to as Glass Reinforced Plastic or GRP), but it is worth mentioning a few others as the choices may come up. Almost all small boats are now built from fibreglass because production costs are low and maintenance is easy. However the life expectancy of a fibreglass hull in water is not infinite, as fibreglass is to varying degrees porous, and water can seep into the hull and expand, causing a nasty condition called osmosis. This is treatable at a price, but it involves some serious digging and re-skinning the hull with a lot of expensive labour. Watch for this on boats that have been kept afloat. There is a preventative measure which is to treat the hull with epoxy, either before it first goes in the water or later on. When my boat had to have the entire hull treated for osmosis, I had the fresh fibreglass covered with an epoxy coat before repainting and going back in the water. I can rest easy knowing she will not get osmosis again, and if I ever sell her, having an epoxy treatment will be a significant selling advantage. Other problems with fibreglass are dulling of the finish over time, which can be corrected with polish and elbow grease, and sometimes crazing of the gel-coat caused by bumps, twists and strains. These and chips or scratches can be easily repaired in warm weather with readily available gel-coat repair kits.

The most common alternative hull and cabin material is the traditional wooden construction. Hulls can be clinker or carvel planked, or what is known as hard chine made of slabs of marine-grade plywood. The hull is usually described by the type of wood. A clinker larch on oak hull would be a planked hull, the planks overlapping rather than smooth, with the planks made of larch and the ribs and frames made of oak. Wood is a lovely traditional material but don't underestimate the amount of maintenance required. It seriously is a lot.

Metal is another material – smaller boats are available in aluminium, larger ones in steel. Both are reasonably easy to maintain. The only other material you may come across is ferro-cement. It is unlikely you will find a ferro-cement boat under nine metres long as they are made of exactly what it says, cement plastered over a ferrous or steel frame. This is a good method of boat-building for one-off, large hulls and many ferro-cement hulls are home-built as with care they are relatively easy to construct. That could be the downside as you have no real guarantee of the build quality for a home-made boat of that size. Unless it is a real bargain I would not really recommend it.

## Where to Buy a Boat

If you decide to go ahead and buy your own boat, take your time and have a good look at what is available. You can buy new, from a dealer or manufacturer, or second hand. Dealers and manufacturers usually have demonstration boats to look at, but this is the most expensive option. Some new boats lose value quickly, although boats from respected manufacturers do not depreciate as much. However, new boats can be customised, and you can be sure there is nothing wrong with them – or if there is, you will have a warranty to cover it. New boats are advertised in boating and angling magazines, and there are boat shows where you can go and compare brands.

The largest boat show is the London Boat Show held every January, formerly at Earls court but currently held in the Docklands area. This is an expensive exhibition, so the smaller manufacturers tend not to exhibit there. The second largest boat show in the UK is the Southampton boat show. Most of the boats are exhibited outdoors or on a temporary marina, so if you go, take a jacket! It is probably the best show for choosing a new angling boat, as most of the manufacturers will be represented. There are other, smaller shows around the country and there are also highly organised Boat Jumbles selling new and second-hand equipment, often selling small boats as well.

One thing to watch with a new boat is the cost. The advertised cost will be for the basic boat, which may or may not include a starter pack of equipment. There is often an additional, and significant, delivery cost and preparation cost, plus antifouling if you are intending to keep the boat afloat. If you are buying new, do take the opportunity of having an epoxy coat applied below the waterline. At this stage of the boats life it will cost a few hundred pounds, but it will save thousands on osmosis treatment later. Unless you are buying a demonstration boat, you will probably have to wait some time for delivery – a few weeks for a small boat, and up to a year for a larger boat from a small manufacturer. Even factory-built boats take time to arrive because many mass-produced boats are manufactured overseas.

Second-hand small boats are advertised in local Trader magazines, angling magazines and in clubs. Larger boats tend to be sold through specialist brokers, in the same way as estate agents sell houses. They have offices in marinas and seaside towns, and advertise in boating magazines. There are an increasing number of web sites dedicated to selling second-hand boats which are a good resource for browsing. Even e-Bay has boats for sale, some of them perfectly acceptable, others highly dubious.

Remember that boats spend much of their time idle, and the rest in one of the most hostile environments on the planet. This means they deteriorate, and unless you know what to look for you should enlist the help of an experienced friend. If you are planning to spend thousands of pounds it is well worth having a professional survey – just as you would when buying a car or house. You can probably recoup the cost of the survey through negotiating the price based on the surveyor's findings.

# Where to Keep Your Boat

After the purchase costs of a boat, storage costs can be the highest financial outlay every year, and where you store your boat can have a great influence on the frequency you use it.

## On a Trailer

Most small boats are kept on a trailer, because their size means they can be kept in an area the size of a large car in a driveway, garden or compound. This has a great advantage in terms of cost and choice of fishing places, but there are downsides. Boats out of the water look surprisingly large, so if you are planning to move a boat into your driveway make sure you have the full agreement and understanding of family and neighbours. Some local planning restrictions may apply to the storage of trailers on your property.

Boats on trailers are very mobile – both for you and for people that may want to remove it without your permission. Also, boats on land are easier to pilfer from so make sure valuables are removed, the engine has a high security lock and the trailer is securely immobilised.

If you are not keeping the trailer on your own property, make sure there is adequate security in the compound, and that your insurance covers the storage area you have chosen.

## Marina Berth

This is probably the most expensive but also the most convenient place to keep your boat. You can keep her afloat, walk right up to her on a pontoon, load her up easily, untie and off you go. When you come back, there are usually extra facilities like a fresh water hose for cleaning, electricity, toilets, showers, shop and a bar. Most good marinas offer parking and 24 hour security surveillance. All this comes at a price, and the demand for marina berths particularly in the South makes this option very expensive, and to keep revenues up many marinas have a minimum charge based on size.

It is worth mentioning a few things to check when you are considering a marina. Once you have a marina berth, you are limiting your fishing to an area within cruising distance from the marina. How long will it take to get from the marina to the fishing ground? As a car travels many times faster than a boat, it is worth finding a marina near a fishing ground even if it is a longer drive to get to the marina.

Although your boat will be afloat all the time in a marina, don't assume you can get in and out of the marina all the time. Because of the tide, and because many marinas are situated in estuaries, there may be a lock or a cill to block the water in to keep the moored boats afloat all the time. A lock allows access at other times, but can be very crowded with long queues at popular times. With a tidal cill, if you are outside when the cill comes up, you stay outside!

Some marinas are more fisherman friendly than others, and it all depends on the commercial management and target "customers". Some marinas are home to expensive cruising and racing yachts, or large power cruisers. Even if you can get an affordable berth in such places, you may find you do not have common interests with other berth holders. In the marina I use, there is a pontoon dedicated to smaller boats and there is quite a camaraderie among follow angling-boat owners, which adds to the pleasure of coming and going from the berth. A quick look at other boats in the marina will give you a good idea how welcome a box of fish on the decking would be.

## Dry Berthing

A popular method of storing small power boats in some marinas is a so-called Dry Berth, which involves storing the boat ashore (in some cases even under cover), and the launching and recovery is done by the marina. All you need to do is phone the marina beforehand, and when you arrive your boat will be floating in the marina. When you come back, you leave it afloat and the marina staff will lift it out and put it into storage. A typical Dry Berth contract will provide 12 months storage and up to 12 launches, you can pay for more as required. This is good for summer anglers, and is cheaper than a standard marina berth for similar facilities. You also save on anti-fouling, which will not be necessary if the boat is kept ashore. The disadvantage is having to pre-book the launch, which you may forget, or change you mind at the last minute if the weather deteriorates. A short two-hour evening trip after work counts as a full launch, so you could easily use up the standard contract launches very quickly.

## Swinging Mooring

Some harbours and rivers offer what is called "swinging moorings", where you rent a mooring buoy and tie your boat up to it so it swings around the buoy with the tide. In more restricted sites, piling berths offer a similar arrangement but the boat is tied fore and aft to two fixed posts. Either way, it is a reasonably economical way to keep the boat afloat. There are several disadvantages however. This type of mooring is the least secure, and insurance premiums will be higher as pilfering and accidental damage from passing boats is more likely. You will also need some means of getting to your boat, so unless there is a local water taxi service you will have to either take a dinghy with you or keep it ashore somewhere nearby, adding to the cost and preparations for a trip.

# Equipment and Safety

Boats need many items of equipment to make sure you can operate them, stay safe, be comfortable and fish effectively. You can spend many happy hours buying and fitting bits and pieces to a boat, and for many, this is all part of the hobby. Boat shows and boat jumbles are a magnet to boat owners – not just for the boats to dream over, but for all the bits and pieces available that are just clamouring for a home on your boat. Most people serving in a yacht chandlers are highly experienced and a mine of information. If you tell them what you need they will be happy to advise the correct size or specification of items so that you buy something suited to your size of boat.

## Safety Regulations

The rules governing the use of pleasure boats at sea are not as obvious, or as rigorously enforced as the rules governing the use of cars on land, but nevertheless they do exist and you need to be aware of the requirements. So far, there are no agencies other than port and harbour authorities and police enforcing these rules in UK waters but if you were involved in an incident and a subsequent investigation found you had not abided by regulations, you could be liable for prosecution or a legal claim.

In 2002 some new regulations came into force which directly affected pleasure boat users. These regulations are part of Chapter Five of the International Convention for the Safety of Life at Sea, which is known as SOLAS V. A leaflet describing the requirements is available from the Maritime and Coastguard Agency. A summary of the requirements are as follows:

- **Weather:** check forecasts before you go out

- **Tides:** check they fit in with what you are planning to do

- **Your boat:** consider whether your boat is suitable for the proposed trip and that you have sufficient safety equipment and fuel with you

- **Your crew:** take into account their experience and physical ability

- **Navigational dangers:** make sure you acquaint yourself with navigational dangers by studying the charts and local almanacs

- **Contingency plan:** always have one should anything go wrong, such as being able to navigate by compass if your GPS fails

- **Information ashore:** make sure someone ashore knows where you are going and when you are expected back, so they can raise the alarm if you do not return as expected

- **Radar reflector:** you are obliged to fit one "if practicable"

- **Life Saving Signals:** you must have access to an illustrated table of the recognised life saving signals such as the one in the Appendices, and study it before you get into trouble

- **Assistance to other craft:** you must inform the Coastguard and any other vessels in the vicinity if you encounter anything that could cause a serious hazard to navigation, and you must respond to a distress signal and help any one or any boat as best you can

- **Misuse of Distress Signals:** Regulation V/35 prohibits the misuse of distress signals, so don't set off flares for fun even in harbour

The following sections cover the basic essentials you need to have on board for safety and navigation. How far you go beyond that is limited only by your budget and interest.

## Safety and Essential Equipment

The RYA, RNLI and Coastguard Services can provide excellent guidance on safety equipment to be carried by private boats, so I will not try and compete with their extensive knowledge and experience. However this book would not be complete without a summary of safety essentials. These are not listed in order of priority – you need all of them.

1. **Personal Flotation Devices.** You must carry some form of flotation assistance for everyone on your boat. Preferably, this would be automatically inflating life jackets that can be worn unobtrusively at all times. I like the "braces" style, you can slip them on and wear them all day without any inconvenience. The advantage of a life jacket is it will keep you floating the right way up for many hours, even if you are unconscious. A buoyancy aid is a very second best, as it will only help you stay afloat rather than keeping you afloat, and even sport ones can be bulky. Buoyancy aids are best kept for rivers and estuaries, and should never be relied on for your personal safety at sea.

2. **Secondary Flotation Devices.** You should also carry a lifebelt or flotation cushion designed for the job. You never know when you might need it, either for a crew member who goes over the side and needs extra help, or for the assistance of someone else already in the water. In addition to the life belt, you also need a floating throwing line. These are usually orange in colour, with

a knot or handle at the end. Both the life belt and throwing rope need to be kept readily accessible – and untangled – because when it is needed, it will be needed in an emergency, when seconds save lives.

3. **Distress Signals.** There are several ways of summoning help of disaster strikes, and you must be acquainted with all of them. All boats should carry a set of distress flares and smoke signals of a type appropriate to the area you fish – you can buy inshore packs, coastal packs and offshore packs in handy watertight containers. They will have expiry dates marked on them, and when that date comes, replace them with new ones. Old flares often fail to ignite or can ignite in a dangerous way, so don't risk it. The Coastguard can dispose of your old flares safely. Don't be tempted to set old ones off on Firework Night, as out-of-date flares can backfire dangerously. I once fired an offshore magnesium flare rocket on the 5th of November, only to see it go up and come straight down again still blazing – right into a neighbour's garden. Luckily no damage was done but it was a salutary lesson. Other forms of distress signal include flames and smoke. If you have room to carry a galvanised metal bucket, you can create an impressive smoke signal by burning oil soaked rags in it – useful as a last resort maybe but not one to be relied upon!

4. **VHF Radio.** Your radio will be a useful means of communication with other boats and the Coastguard, but as an item of safety equipment it has no equal. All boats should carry a VHF set, preferably a fixed set run from the boat electrics and a second, hand-held set as a backup. All VHF sets must be licensed to the boat, and all operators must be qualified, or supervised by a qualified operator. This means taking some training, sitting a short operator's examination and obtaining a VHF Operators Certificate. This is a one-off cost; the boat VHF licence has to be renewed annually.

   **Digital Selective Calling (DSC) radios** will soon become obligatory, and are worth installing correctly. DSC radios have many advantages including being able to signal specific boats like a telephone, but their main safety advantage is that they can be connected to a GPS so that the current position of the set can be broadcast automatically – a great safety asset in an emergency. DSC sets have a red "panic button" which transmits an emergency message identifying the vessel and position, which is often the most difficult (and important) bit to get right when communicating verbally in an emergency.

5. **Bilge pump and bailer.** Your boat may already be fitted with a pump to remove water from inside, if not you must fit one. If it is electrically powered then it is advisable to have a manual pump as well, in case flooding damages the electrical circuits. If

you leave your boat afloat, fit a float switch to start the pump if the water level rises inside the boat, this can deal with rainwater flooding or minor leaks that could sink a boat over time. In addition, you should also carry strong plastic buckets. These have many uses, particularly on an angling boat, and will be invaluable if you have to chuck water over the side in a hurry.

6. **Tools and repair "bits".** You could easily go over the top with tools and repair materials. In an emergency, there are limited repairs you can do yourself when at sea, but if you can do some minor repairs you might prevent a situation developing into something worse, or you might be able to keep fishing instead of abandoning a day. Buy a large plastic food-saver type box with a tightly fitting lid, and keep the following items on board. Spray any metal tools with WD-40 even if they claim to be stainless.

- Heavy duty pliers
- Long-nose pliers
- Large screwdrivers
    (cross-head and Phillips)
- Electrical screwdriver
- Tube of caulk
- Adjustable spanner
- Plug spanner
    (for petrol engines)
- Shackle key
- Assortment of strong twine

- Stainless wire
- Assortment of electrical cable of
    the type used in your boat's
    wiring loom
- Appropriate fuses and spare
    bulbs
- Stainless screws, nuts, washers
    and bolts
- Tin of WD-40
- Electrical tape
- Electrical connectors

7. **Powerful torch.** You may not plan to be out at night but if you end up that way, you'll need a torch.

8. **Mobile Phone.** I hesitated in including this, as it implies that it can be used in place of your VHF for emergencies. Although a mobile phone can be used to reach the coastguard on 999, you may not be in an area with good signal coverage. More importantly however, the coastguard cannot obtain a directional position fix on a phone, which means that if you are not sure exactly where you are, they cannot locate you. There was a tragedy near Morecambe where a father and son were able to contact the coastguard by phone, but because of the fog, their position could not be fixed. Both were drowned. Having said that, I would still ensure I had a mobile phone with me, just in case there were transmission problems on VHF. You never know.

9. **Anchor.** Unless you plan to fish only on the drift, you will have an anchor on board anyway, and you will take this aspect of your boat's equipment more seriously than the average speedboat owner. Anchors are essential safety items as well, as they can prevent you getting into serious problems if your engine fails

close to rocks, sandbanks or busy shipping channels. There are several different types of anchor available, all with their own advantages, so the choice is yours. I would recommend carrying a spare, in case the first does not hold in an emergency, and also in case you lose one while fishing. Carrying a spare means you can carry on fishing. See the section on Anchoring for more information on anchors and anchor rope.

10. **Rope.** In a list of safety equipment, rope is for repairs, towing or tying to a rescue boat. Your anchor rope will make a good tow rope, so make sure it can be used in that way by being quickly unshackled from the anchor chain. Your mooring ropes, if they are of a sensible length, will also serve as emergency ropes for a variety of purposes.

11. **Secondary means of propulsion.** Depending on the size of your boat, this could be a paddle, oars, small outboard or second engine. This is not always practical, and there are many commercial boats relying on a single engine. However, it is always preferable to have a backup, particularly if you are relying on a petrol engine or outboard as these are more prone to failure than a marine diesel engine.

12. **Navigation lights.** If you intend to fish at night or into winter evenings, you must equip your boat with navigation lights according to the Rules of the Road. (See section on Navigation Lights). Even if you do not plan to be out late, a problem may delay your return and you must show navigation lights so other boats can see you and avoid a collision. If you do not fit permanent navigation lights, you can buy battery powered emergency navigation lights for small boats from a good yacht chandlers. For small motor boats and dinghies under 7 metres in length and a maximum speed of 7 knots, the minimum is a white light visible all the way round, mounted on a short mast. Motor boats under 50 metres in length must show a white light visible from ahead (steaming light), a white light visible from astern (stern light), and a green starboard light visible from ahead and a red port light visible from ahead. Boats under 12 metres in length can combine the forward and stern white lights into a single white light visible all round. Boats at anchor must show a single white light visible all round.

13. **Anchor Ball.** All boats at anchor must show during daylight hours a black ball hoisted in the forward rigging, or on a pole over the front part of the boat. A spherical ball is bulky to stow, so a convenient alternative is two flat black disks that can be slotted together when in use to appear as a ball, and can be stored flat.

**14. Horn.** This is used for signalling your intentions, such as turning to port or starboard, and also for attracting attention in an emergency. If you do not have an electric horn fitted to your boat, you can buy an air-canister horn (as used at football matches) very cheaply at a yacht chandlers. If you do not use air horns regularly, check them because they can leak, and an empty air canister will not make a noise just when you may need it.

# Navigation Equipment

There are some navigation items I would consider essential, some desirable and some are luxury items. However it does depend where you are fishing – a radar set for example would be a luxury item in Southampton Water but essential for mid-channel wrecking.

## Essential

1. **Compass.** Every boat must have a compass, properly adjusted for the boat's own magnetic influences, and you need to know how to use it. By far the best way to learn how to use a compass is to attend a navigation course such as those run by the RYA.

2. **Detailed charts** of the areas you will be travelling and fishing in. On the same navigation courses, you will learn how to read these maps of the sea, and understand the information they contain. Admiralty charts are the best, and they also produce Leisure editions for non-commercial users.

3. **Echo sounder/fish-finder.** Knowing the depth of water is vital, both for fishing and for safety. As you are running a boat primarily for fishing, a good fish-finder will be high on your shopping list anyway, for identifying good fish-holding features. As a safety aid it is invaluable, for warning you of dangerously shallow water, and for confirming your estimated position. If you think you are in a position which according to your chart has 20 metres of water but your echo sounder shows significantly different, you know you will have to re-check your position.

Tips:

Keep a notebook or loose-leaf plastic wallet containing details of marks, contact numbers, articles from magazines, printouts from web sites, minimum fish sizes etc.

Keep your notebook, pencil, rubber, charts, tidal atlas and equipment instruction books in a splash-proof satchel of the type commonly given away at conferences. That way everything is to hand and you are less likely to forget odds and ends when you go fishing.

## Highly Desirable

1. **A GPS set** is very useful, but not essential. In fact, it is a good idea to get used to navigating without a GPS, firstly because you would look very stupid if it failed and you were lost despite having a compass and charts on board, and secondly because a GPS only takes account of positions and directions. It does not take account of wind and tide, both of which are very influential and for effective navigation, particularly over long distances, you need to understand and make allowances for their effects. Modern GPS sets are amazingly accurate and relatively cheap compared to their predecessors. For identification of positions and basic directional navigation, a hand held set is quite adequate. A fixed set will have a larger screen and a useful tracking facility, which allows you to back-track over marks you may have spotted on the fish-finder, or to replicate effective drifts.

2. **Tidal Atlas.** For the price (currently less than £10), this little booklet should be in every skipper's navigation bag. Tidal Atlases are published by the same Admiralty publications body as Admiralty Charts, and are available from good yacht chandlers. They show tidal currents in terms of direction and relative strength for every hour of the tide, and make it very easy to plan where to fish to take advantage of tide strength and direction over marks. For navigation purposes, it is a much easier way of estimating the effect of tidal currents on your boat's progress through the water than working it out from the tables printed on Admiralty charts.

## Luxury Items

1. **Chart Plotter.** I see a lot of these fitted in small boats, and there is no denying that they combine chart information and GPS positions in a very visual and easy to use way. But again, they should never take the place of compass, chart and GPS because if you rely on them and they fail, you are in trouble. It also tempts you to jump in, switch on and go, without taking the trouble to learn the basics of navigation and seamanship. You need those basics to get the most out of advanced navigation equipment like a chart plotter.

2. **Radar.** These are now available in small sizes suitable for small boats, and no longer drain batteries like the old sets used to. Invaluable for long distance work, and where you are likely to be near busy shipping lanes, for the small boat operator they are useful but not really essential. If you do decide to install a set, don't underestimate the amount of time you need to spend learning to operate them. A course on electronic navigation equipment is well worth the investment.

You will doubtless make your own list of items that you feel you need for your boat, and that list will grow with each visit to a yacht chandler or boat show. Here is a list of items that I would recommend you start with for a five metre outboard powered fishing boat, and you can add to it as you wish.

# Other Equipment

1. **Mooring ropes.** These are useful for tying up alongside a jetty, and for manoeuvring a boat onto a trailer. There are many different types of rope, but the best for mooring ropes are braided, which feel soft, and made of nylon or polyester. Don't skimp on the length, you may have to tie up to a bollard some distance away so make sure you have at least three ropes of 10 metres each, or more for a larger boat.

2. **Fenders.** These hang over the side to protect your boat from banging against a harbour wall or another boat. You should have at least three each side, with fender eyes screwed to your boat at strategic points to tie them on to if your boat does not have safety rails in convenient places. Fenders are not usually supplied with ropes so you need a short rope of a suitable diameter so you can tie the fender to your boat, and adjust the height to suit whatever you are bumping against.

3. **Boat hook.** Useful for hooking up ropes, mooring buoys, lost odds and ends, and hooking on or fending off as you manoeuvre alongside a jetty or another boat.

4. **Spare fuel can (full).** Self explanatory, unless you have a very large built-in fuel tank with an external fuel gauge. It is a good idea to have a spare can of the same capacity as your main fuel tank, so if you inadvertently allow it to run dry, you will probably have enough in your second can to get back home.

5. **Second battery.** Batteries can and do run flat, particularly if you operate a lot of equipment and lights from your main battery. You will not be able to start a large outboard or an inboard without a well charged battery, so it is highly advisable to have two batteries, one for engine starting and the other for operating what is called the "domestic" system. These can be switched so the engine battery is isolated while fishing, and both charged while under way.

6. **Storage.** This all depends on your boat design, but all the equipment listed so far that is not screwed to the boat, needs to be kept somewhere. Storage bays and seat lockers are invaluable, but if you do not have these, then invest in plastic storage boxes with lids. If you holiday in the USA, buy a couple of the large, chest-style cool boxes from a supermarket. They are ideal for storage as well as keeping bait and fish fresh. They are much cheaper in the USA compared to here and can easily be checked

in with your luggage on the way home. You should also fit hooks, racks and holders to keep things like rods, gaffs, landing net, boathook, paddle etc. from rolling about. Plenty of rings fixed to the boat and some elasticated luggage hooks (with plastic hooks) makes it a lot easier to keep things together. If you don't, then the first few waves will make a complete mess in your boat and the next few could flip them over the side.

---

Tip:
Don't bother with those blue plastic freezer blocks for your cool-box. Firstly get a big cool-box (for all those fish), and almost fill two or three two-litre drink bottles with water. Freeze them solid and use them instead of freezer blocks - they will last all day and keep your catch as fresh as the commercial fishermen do – on ice.

---

7. **Bait cutting board.** It is worth making up something specifically for managing bait on board, as a small boat tossing about at sea is no place for a loose board, knives and bits of bait. Boats designed for angling sometimes have storage boxes with lids made of cutting board material, which are ideal. Alternatively you could fix a section of plastic chopping board to the boat transom, or make up a detachable one to fix to the gunwales. A secure place to hold the bait cutting knife makes sure it doesn't get lost or inadvertently cause someone some harm.

8. **Rod holders.** These are well worth fitting, and adjustable ones can hold rods for transport as well as holding rods while fishing. If you are fishing alone with several rods or trolling, these are essential. It is advisable to secure the rod with a lanyard even if there is a locking device, as a large fish or a snagged line while the boat is moving could snap the rod holder before the line breaks. A lanyard will stop you losing the rod as well.

9. **Grab handles.** The old seafaring adage "one hand for the ship and one for yourself" is true enough. When you move around in the boat, whether you are under way or fishing, you are on a very unstable platform and it is all too easy to fall and hurt yourself, or worse, fall over the side. If your boat is not fitted with enough hand-holds, buy some handles or handrails from a yacht chandlers and fit them yourself. Use through-bolts, not screws, and pad the underside of the fibreglass with a plate of plywood to spread the load. You don't want the handrail pulling off just when you have grabbed it to save yourself.

# Launching and Recovering

If you trail your boat, then how easy it is to get it into and out of the water will make the difference between a fun day and a miserable one. Here are a few tips to help. The description is based on a typical five metre outboard powered angling boat, if you have anything significantly different then not all the details will apply.

## The Launch Site

If you can, find a wide, concrete slipway that is neither too steep or too shallow, in a location sheltered from wind and tidal currents, accessible at all states of the tide, wide enough for several boats, ample parking nearby and near good fishing marks. If one exists in the UK with all those features I am not aware of it. Usually there is a compromise somewhere, so it is a good idea to research your launch site at high tide and low tide before you use it. A chat with someone already using the slipway will give you a lot of vital information. Make sure your towing vehicle has enough traction to pull a loaded trailer back up the ramp, and that there is enough slipway under the water to support your trailer when immersed. Some have a nasty "trailer-trap" of a sharp drop-off just out of sight, and if your trailer wheels go over the edge, getting the trailer back again could be a challenge.

Some slipways end in shingle or "hard", which sometimes is not, or at least some of it may be soft. Check it out before driving your car down, even a 4x4 will get bogged in loose shingle.

Tip:
Trailers differ in style and price, and if you plan to launch regularly from slipways it is worth investing in the type of trailer that has a rear section that swings or swivels, to help align the boat onto the trailer when recovering. This type of trailer can also save your trailer wheel bearings as they can allow the boat to slide off more easily, so you do not have to reverse so far into the water.

## Launching

As most ramps are wide enough for only one trailer at a time, it is polite to get in and out as quickly as possible to let others launch as well. When you arrive, do a quick recce and check with other slipway users to see if there is any useful news, like an unexpected obstruction or loose shingle swept across the concrete by a storm. You may also need to pay any fees due, which may include both slipway fees and harbour dues. Park up in a position where you can reverse down the slipway, but out of the way from other users. You can now remove the trailer lighting board, load straps and other ties, and get everything ready. Ensure drain plugs are securely in. It is worth making your own checklist to make sure you do not forget something vital, like connecting the fuel line to the outboard!

This pause for preparation has another vital function. The trailer wheel hubs will be hot from the journey, and if they are dipped in cold water the sudden temperature change will cause the hubs to suck water past the bearing seals and into the bearings. The only way to avoid this is to fit "bearing savers" which create a permanent pressure on the bearing grease so they do not suck in water. The disadvantage of these is that there is a tendency for grease to be forced out if the seals are anything but perfect, and if you have a braked trailer this can wreck the brake pads. Avoid the so-called "sealed for life" bearings, these are very expensive to replace and as they cannot be disassembled for maintenance they can fail without warning.

Slipways can be slimy, covered in shingle and fairly steep. Your car brakes and wheel grip may not be sufficient to hold everything steady if you stop on the slope, so it is a very good idea to have a couple of sturdy wooden blocks handy, to use as chocks under the wheels. Use oak or a similar hardwood for strength, drill a hole through them and attach a short length of floating rope, preferably of a bright colour. This makes it safer to pull away from under the wheels, and colourful rope will help you remember to pick them up afterwards. Floating rope will help you find them if they end up in muddy water!

Before reversing into the water, make sure the boat will not slide off the trailer before you mean it to, and have a rope tied ready to the bow to secure the boat as soon as it is in the water. Have someone hold the rope and watch behind you to make sure the slipway is clear. Reversing a trailer is often thought to be difficult but it need not be. The trick is not to think about it. Your elongated "vehicle" has a hinge in the middle, it is pushing instead of pulling, and steers from the back. You can try and work out which direction to steer but it is much easier with the following method. Start off with the boat and car aligned straight, and keeping your eyes on the boat, either directly or via the mirrors, reverse very slowly in the direction you want to go. If the back of the boat wanders to the side, very gently turn the steering wheel. If that makes it worse, turn it gently the other way. You will very quickly work out which way to turn the steering wheel to make the trailer go where you want it to.

Reverse down the ramp as far as necessary to either slide or float the boat off, preferably without putting your trailer wheel bearings under water, and definitely without getting your car wet. Have your assistant pull the boat away from the slipway and either beach it or tie up to something to allow others to use the slipway, while the car and trailer is parked and secured. Always have someone by the boat as a rising tide or wash from a passing ship could easily float it away. Conversely a dropping tide can leave it stranded and impossible to move until the water returns.

Moving off is simple if the beach shelves steeply and there are no cross-winds or currents. However if there is a cross-wind or current you will need to reverse out promptly otherwise you will be swept, probably sideways, into the beach or slipway. The trick is to get everything prepared, then make the final move as one slick operation. Firstly get someone aboard and while the boat is steadied, put the engine down, if there is enough water to do this, and start the engine. Make sure it is running smoothly and check cooling water is circulating and coming out of the indicator tube. Get everyone else aboard except the person holding the boat, and align the boat at 90° to the shore with an oar or boathook. The assistant now needs to scramble in (waders and a boarding ladder come in useful here unless they are athletic and enjoy being wet), while you reverse directly and purposefully away. Keep the oar or boathook handy because if the engine cuts or the propeller fouls a rope at this point, you can get quickly and safely back again to sort the problem out. Be very careful of underwater obstructions, because the first part of your boat to meet them will be your revolving propeller, and the engine is designed to kick up to minimise impact damage only when going ahead.

## Returning and Recovering the Boat

After your trip, the recovery sequence is almost exactly the reverse of the launch sequence. Gently nose your boat ashore if the beach is soft, or tie up nearby if there is a jetty available. Stop the engine, get everyone out and tilt the engine to keep the propeller out of harms way when you put the boat on the trailer. Reverse the car and trailer down the slipway and guide the boat onto the trailer. On a steep ramp you may be able to float the boat on all the way, otherwise you will have to use the trailer winch. If there is a cross-wind or current pushing the boat out of alignment, getting the thin point of the keel onto the trailer rollers can be very tricky. If you keep two of your mooring ropes tied one at each side of the stern, you can use two helpers to keep the boat aligned by pulling on the ropes. In muddy water you may not be able to see whether the boat is aligned correctly over the trailer rollers, so drive slowly forward a few feet, if the boat is not on properly go back and try again. Don't drive too far up the ramp when doing this as the boat may be touching some part of the trailer that will cause damage if the full weight of the boat rests on it.

Once you are sure the boat is on, secure the boat to make sure it will not slip off the back of the trailer and drive up the ramp to a clear space where you can get everything ready for the road. Open drain plugs, tidy loose items away and secure everything with ties and ropes. Make sure you fit an additional brace to keep the outboard motor propped up, on some models a simple wooden block will do the job, as the boat bouncing on a trailer can easily dislodge or break the standard outboard motor tilt clips.

Tips:

There are two modifications worth making to your trailer. The first is to fit two vertical metal rods sticking up above the trailer wheel axle, wide enough to clear the sides of the boat and high enough to see above water when you are guiding the boat onto the trailer. If you can, make these rods sturdy enough so they can hold the boat aligned correctly above the trailer once the boat is between them. This saves a lot of trouble when you have a difficult cross-wind or current to contend with.

The second tip is to fit a sturdy flat board to your trailer drawbar using galvanised U-bolts, so you can walk along the trailer from the shore to the boat, to make adjustments or connect the winch hook. This is much easier than stumbling through the water, potentially tripping over bits of submerged trailer. Cover the top of the board with some form of non-slip surface so you are less likely to fall off it.

# Boat Handling – Under Way

This may seem strange, but making a boat go where you want it to on the water is not as simple as steering it like a car. It does not have wheels that grip a road, or rails to run on. It floats on a moving substance, and is under the influence of wind and wave without anything to hold it firmly in position or even facing in any particular direction. Knowing what your boat will do when you move off, steer it, or stop will make the difference between staying in control – or not.

A light boat, particularly one with very little hull surface under the waterline, will be very difficult to steer at very low speeds. All boats need some forward movement to create the turning effect caused by movement of the rudder or outboard. You will need to experiment to find the minimum speed that you can maintain and still steer the boat.

The tide or current will affect your boat's movement over the sea-bed, because the boat is suspended in a body of water which itself is moving bodily over the ground. You need to take account of this, particularly when travelling across a river or harbour mouth, as you will in effect slide sideways from your intended path. At least this is reasonably predictable and you can allow for it, unlike the wind which has an annoying tendency to gust.

Wind causes more bumps and scrapes when boat handling than any other influence. Light boats, particularly those with a shallow draft and a sharply raked bow are very prone to being pushed by the wind, and instead of being a neat sideways push, the wind will vary in strength, catch you out with sudden gusts, and also try and swivel the boat around the part most deeply set in the water. Knowing what your boat will do when the wind blows is more than half the problem solved. When you know what the boat will do you can anticipate it and even use it to your advantage.

It is a good idea to take a new boat off to a quiet spot in a harbour or estuary and experiment with slow speeds, putting the engine in neutral, watching what happens when the wind catches the bows from either side, and generally becoming familiar with the way the boat behaves. Most outboard and out-drive powered boats will tend to drift stern to wind, because the leg will create more drag than any other part of the hull. When you stop the boat for drift fishing for example, it is useful to know this in advance because you can head the boat away from the wind as you cut the engine, which means you can start drift fishing immediately without lines tangling as the boat turns.

Another effect worth knowing about is the torque created by the rotation of the propeller. This applies to all propellers except duo-props. The rotation of a normal propeller "winds" the stern sideways as well as pushing the water behind it. This torque has little effect when cruising, but makes quite a difference to slow speed handling. When turning sharply at any speed you will notice that the boats turns more sharply in one direction than the other. Remember which way is the tighter turn and allow for it when making turns in one direction or another. If your boat is fitted with two engines, with propellers rotating in opposite directions, the torque effect on one propeller is cancelled by the other so the boat will handle more evenly when under power from both engines. When torque is needed, it can be brought into play by manoeuvring with one engine or another. A twin-engined boat in the hands of a skilled helmsman can be made to do some remarkable things!

The torque effect can help you in some very tight places. If you need to turn the boat round in a very narrow channel such as in a marina, you can use the torque to push the stern sideways. If you put the engine in gear and blip the throttle with the helm hard over, the stern will make a distinctive lateral movement before there is any significant forward movement. If you turn the helm hard over in the other direction and blip the throttle in reverse, you will cancel the forward movement and kick the stern in the same direction as before. By repeating this several times, you can turn a boat around in its own length – very useful where there is no room for a three point turn!

# Boat Handling – Mooring

You may be keeping your boat in a marina, or you may only occasionally moor alongside a pontoon or harbour wall. Either way, you need to know how to do this properly to make sure your boat is secure and will not swing about causing damage to your boat or others.

This section covers mooring ropes and methods used for approaching and leaving the pontoon. Types of ropes available, and instructions on how to tie the knots mentioned are contained in the section on Ropes and Knots.

## Ropes and Cleats

Your boat needs to have at least five tying up points, regardless of size: one at the bows, one at each stern quarter, and one either side amidships. There is a reason for having all these, as you will see later. The most common form of securing point is a cleat, and you should fit the largest you can, within reason. You will probably need to tie several ropes onto a single cleat sooner or later, which is next to impossible on an undersized cleat. Your bow cleat should be particularly large, and most new boats are supplied with pathetically small ones. The bow cleat takes a lot of strain, as it acts as a mooring point, anchoring point and possibly a tow point. All cleats must be through-bolted with a strengthening pad underneath to spread the load.

If your mooring point is inboard from the gunwales you will probably have fairleads to guide the ropes over the side. These are not necessary if the cleat is fitted right at the edge of the deck. Often you will find fairleads at the bows only.

Ropes for tying up are referred to as mooring warps or dock lines. The most suitable material is nylon or polyester; braided is nicer to handle but more expensive than three strand. You need at least three mooring warps, preferably more, and at least two of them should be double the length of your boat. This is because you may need to double up on a rope to create a slip rope, or you may need to allow for the tide to drop if you are not tied up to a floating pontoon.

Tip:

Splice or tie a loop at one end of each mooring warp, and make the size of the loop fairly generous. This makes it much easier to slip the line over a bollard and quickly get a secure point ashore when you are coming alongside. You can concentrate on tidying up your mooring once you are connected with dry land. Large loops can slip off however, so if you are using it to tie up for any length of time, use the loop to create a noose, or if the mooring point ashore is a cleat with a hole in the middle, run the line through the hole first then loop back over the cleat.

To secure your boat to a pontoon, you need a line from the bows to a point forward of the boat, a line from the stern to a point astern of the boat, and lines called "springs" from the points where you moored the bow and stern lines to points at the opposite ends of the boat, for example the bow or fore spring will be connected from the bow to a point on the pontoon amidships or astern. These springs create a triangulation effect which as we know from our maths lessons is the most stable shape, and will prevent your boat swinging backwards and forwards, in and out.

Another line, called a "breast rope" is useful, which leads from the point amidships of your boat to a point on the pontoon directly opposite. This keeps the boat in close to the pontoon but as it is short and at 90° to the boat and pontoon, it does not allow for any boat movement as the tide changes or the boat load changes as people get in and out, so make sure it is not so tight it strains the cleat.

Knowing which knots to use is important because you want your boat to be secure, but it must also be possible to untie a knot easily even after you have pulled it very tight. If you have cleats on your boat and ashore, the best way is the "figure of eight" the rope over the cleat two or three times, and then put another turn on but this time tucking the free end (tail) under the final loop. With practice you can do this by twisting your wrist on the final loop and the tail will be neatly secured.

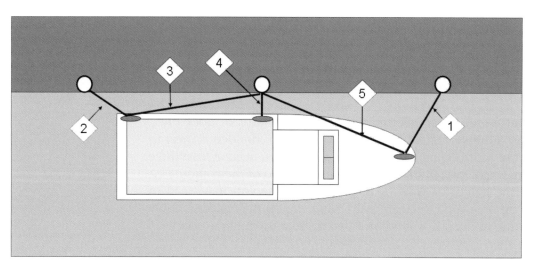

1. Bow line
2. Stern line
3. Stern (aft) spring
4. Breast line
5. Bow (fore) spring

**Mooring Lines**

If you are tying up to a bollard, ring or post, the best knot to use is a round turn and two half hitches. The round turn takes much of the strain, leaving the two half hitches to secure the rope. This means the hitches are less likely to tighten up under load so they can be more easily untied. See the section on Ropes and Knots for more details.

Once the boat is secure, the final check is to adjust the fenders that protect your boat from rubbing on the hard pontoon or jetty wall. A clove hitch is the best knot to attach the fender tail rope to a handrail, as that is easily adjusted for height. It is a good idea to leave some fenders out on the other side of the boat, as it is common practice in busy harbours for other boats to tie up alongside your own if they is no room directly alongside the pontoon. Tidy the ropes and coil loose ends neatly – it not only looks good, it will prevent someone tripping on them.

## Moving Off

If you had the harbour to yourself, there was no wind, there was no tide and there were plenty of helpers on board and on shore, leaving the pontoon would be so easy. Untie, push off and away you go. Unfortunately, that happy state rarely occurs so you will have to know a few tricks so you can slip neatly away without embarrassing bumps and scrapes.

The first step before moving off is to remove your springs and the breast line. That is referred to as "singling up", leaving a single line fore and aft. With no contrary wind and tides, you can usually hold a light boat in place with a boathook, untie the mooring lines, push the boat away from the pontoon and motor slowly away. If you turn the wheel sharply, as you will probably have to, to clear other vessels, watch the stern as it will probably swing wide and knock the pontoon. This is where the fenders and boathook come in handy again.

If you have a strong wind or tide to contend with, moving away will be more difficult as the natural forces will be trying to push your boat somewhere else. With care however, these forces can be used to help rather than hinder.

If tide or wind are pushing from ahead, remove the stern line first, motor gently ahead to slacken the bow line and keep the boat under control, then remove the bow line before moving away. If you don't have a helper ashore, run the bow line round the bollard and back to the boat so you can untie one end and pull the line back round the bollard with the other, without leaving the boat. If the wind or tide are pushing from astern, do exactly the same but with the stern line.

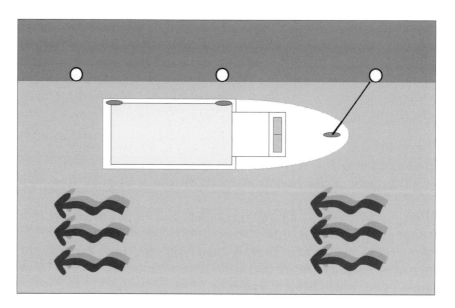

**Moving Off – 1**

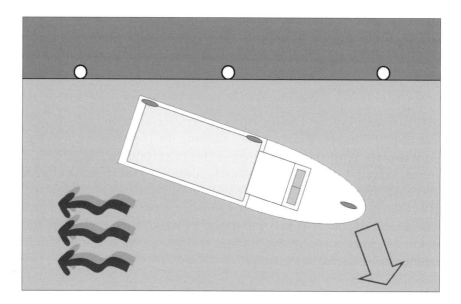

**Moving Off – 2**

If you have very little room between your boat and others tied up, moving away can be tricky because wind or tide can push your boat into others before you can move away, and sometimes there is so little room the turning circle of your boat may be too large for the space available. This is where another little trick using the mooring lines comes in.

If the wind or current are pushing the boat from ahead, untie all mooring lines except the bow line. The bow line should be attached to a bollard well forward of the bows if that is possible. It will also help if you run the bow line round the bollard and back to the boat, but secure it with a figure of eight around a cleat as it will be put under more than usual strain with this manoeuvre and you need to be able to release it afterwards.

You boat will now be lying to a single mooring point, and kept in position against the pontoon by the strength of the current or wind. To move out, under perfect control, put the engine in reverse at tick-over speed, and gently turn the wheel away from the pontoon. You may need to experiment with the engine revs and the amount of wheel movement, but make every adjustment very gradual. You should be able to swing the entire boat out from the pontoon like a giant pendulum. When the boat is clear of other boats, put the engine in neutral, quickly untie the bow line and pull it back into

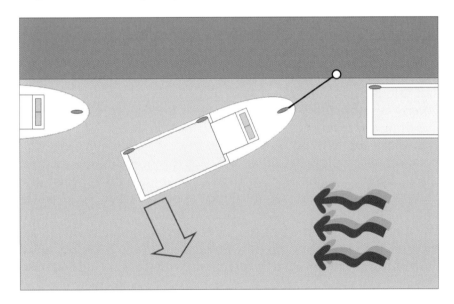

**Moving Off From a Congested Mooring**

the boat, and reverse gently away from the pontoon. Once fully clear you can put the engine in forward gear, straighten up and away you go. This will look very impressive to the casual bystander.

If your boat is being pushed from wind or tide from astern, carry out exactly the same pendulum manoeuvre, but this time securing from the stern to a point behind the boat, but this time you will be moving out forwards. You can also use this method when there is no tide but a strong wind is pushing you back against the pontoon.

# Coming Alongside

Coming alongside a pontoon is made more difficult because usually you will not have much time to check out wind, tide, mooring points and other boats' activities, so you will have to make some quick checks and quick decisions. Before you get near the pontoon, put fenders out on both sides, secure a mooring line on the forward, stern and mid-ships cleats and have the lines coiled neatly where they will not get tangled or trodden on.

It is important to stay in complete control of the boat, so you don't have to rush anything. One sure way of keeping control is to head the boat into the wind or current. That way the forward movement of the boat will be balanced by the pressure of wind and current, and if they can be made equal, the boat can be held in a stable position. If you have the wind or current behind you and you are moving forwards, you will end up going twice as fast as you meant to and probably end up hitting something expensive.

If you have plenty of room on the pontoon, come towards it at your slowest speed that still gives you control, against the direction of wind or tide, at an angle of about 45° or less to the pontoon. At the last minute, turn your wheel to straighten up and put the engine in reverse to stop the boat. This is where knowledge of your boat handling characteristics will make this last bit easier. A boat is not on wheels or rails, so it has a tendency to slide sideways. The rotation of the propeller drives the boat forwards, but the rotation also creates a slight sideways kick, more noticeable when the throttle is given a burst, and the direction of the kick will depend on whether the propeller is rotating clockwise or anticlockwise. You can use this to good effect when you are coming alongside to nudge the stern in towards the pontoon, without driving the bows out away from it. You will need to experiment with forward and reverse bursts, and a port or starboard helm, but once you know which one to use it is very helpful. On my boat for example, I know that when coming alongside with a pontoon on the port side, by turning the wheel towards the pontoon as I give the engine a burst of reverse to stop the boat, the stern swings neatly in to straighten the boat up against the pontoon.

Once you are alongside, the boat must be quickly secured so it does not drift away from the pontoon – which it would quickly do. If you have enough help available, get a line ashore and secured at the bows and stern, and adjust the lines and add springs later. If you are on your own, or the conditions are particularly difficult, having a line secured at one end of the boat does not really solve the problem, particularly if the current or wind catches the boat and swings it out from the pontoon. In these circumstances, I like to get a breast rope secured first – it may not look too neat but it keeps the

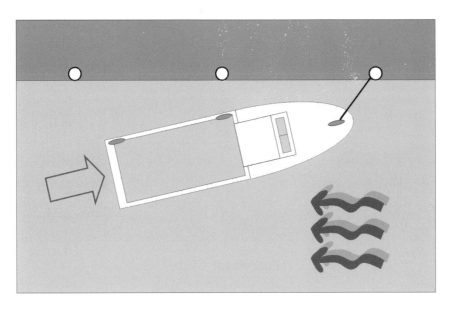

**Coming Alongside**

boat in one place and it cannot swing out from the pontoon. You can add and adjust lines at your leisure once you are securely joined on to the shore.

There are two more techniques that will help you come alongside when conditions are crowded or currents are strong. The first of these is called the "ferry boat glide".

If you are coming alongside a pontoon where the tide is exceptionally strong and there is little room for error on the pontoon, such as where there are other boats moored ahead and astern of your chosen spot, motor gently up heading into the current approaching your mooring position by steering close but perfectly parallel to the pontoon. When you are exactly opposite your berth, reduce the engine throttle so that you only just have enough forward momentum to remain stationery, held there by the current. By moving your wheel fractionally towards the pontoon you will be able to move sideways into your berth. Be ready to reduce speed further as you move between other boats as the current is likely to be weaker at that point. You can use the same method for coming up to a mooring buoy – align yourself alongside it then just slide the boat sideways to allow someone to catch it from the bows.

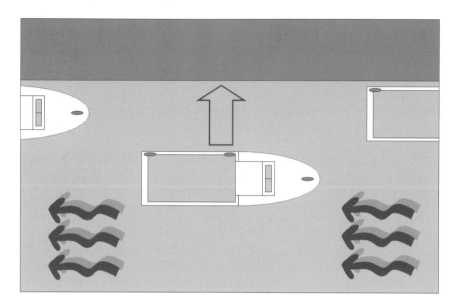

**Ferryboat Glide**

This takes a bit of practice, but again, if you know what your boat does when you turn the wheel or increase engine revolutions, you can use it to your advantage when manoeuvring. Take time to practice in a harbour, estuary or marina, it will be well worth it when you have to come alongside a busy pontoon with a gawping audience on the shore!

The second technique involves mooring a boat alongside a pontoon with a single rope. This can be used as part of a more complex manoeuvre, or as a temporary hold. If you attach a bow spring only, you can hold a boat against the pontoon by going ahead very gently and turning the wheel away from the pontoon. The spring will hold the bows against the pontoon, the engine will hold the stern in. Again, you will have to work out how much engine and how much wheel is needed for your particular boat, but I have seen this method used as a regular way of making a temporary mooring by the ferry operators who travel the fiords in Norway like a water-bus, stopping every mile or two to pick up drop off passengers from isolated communities. A single mooring line with a large loop makes coming alongside a quick and secure process.

Tip:

Keep looking around you, particularly when going astern. I have seen some very expensive boats reverse right into other boats because the helmsman was more worried about avoiding something in front of him.

# Boat Handling – At Sea

One you are under way and ready to take to open water, there is another complication that Nature will put in your way – waves. Waves are not as simple as they seem from the shore, and need a bit of understanding to make boat handling easier.

## Waves

Waves have a height, measured from peak to trough. They also have a length, from peak to peak. A wave with a long wavelength compared to the height is called a swell, and a short wavelength creates what is referred to as a "short" sea. A swell, even a large one, can make for a smooth ride but a short sea can be very uncomfortable indeed as the boats bows will dig in or slam against the side of the wave.

Normal waves are created by and pushed by the wind, and the effect is to make the slope on the side the wind is blowing from more gentle, and the slope on the side the wind is blowing to, more steep. This can catch you out, because if you are heading out to sea with a strong wind blowing from astern, you may think the sea is quite manageable. When you turn and head back, you will find a very different situation as you are now heading into the steep side of the wave and you may have to slow down considerably to make safe headway.

Waves advance along the open sea in the direction the wind is blowing, in rows at right angles to the direction of the wind. When they reach shallow water, or where the wind changes direction around a headland, waves can also change direction. When they meet an obstruction such as the shore, they will bounce off at an angle. In enclosed waters near shore and around islands, waves can be going in many directions at once, and as they intersect, the surface of the water becomes very confused and choppy.

A wave moves along the surface of the water but the water itself does not move along – in fact the particles of water make a circle on the vertical plane. If you float on the water without wind and tide you just move up and down – waves in open water will only move you as you slide down the side of a wave. As soon as a wave reaches a depth of water shallower than that required for the free rotation of the water particles, the wave will break at the top.

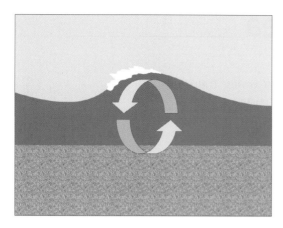

That is why you will see shallow water shown up by waves breaking over them, even though there may still be water covering the bottom. Small waves will only break in very shallow water, larger waves will break in proportionately deeper water. This is not to be confused with waves breaking caused by very strong winds – refer to the section on the Beaufort Scale for indicators of wind strength.

Waves also change their form when the wind blows across a body of moving water, such as a tidal current. Wind blowing in the same direction as the tidal current will tend the flatten the waves, wind blowing against the tidal current will make the waves steeper. This can create a potentially dangerous situation for a small boat, where you may be fishing in a gentle wave with wind over tide, but as the tide turns and becomes wind against tide, the waves can become very nasty within minutes – particularly in areas where the tide runs hard.

If you get caught out and have to head for home facing into a steep sea, the wave height and steep angle can be very uncomfortable or even dangerous, forcing you to slow down considerably. In these circumstances it is safer to travel at an angle to the waves rather than straight into them, which means you will not be going up and down such a steep gradient and the boat will roll gently over the wave crest rather than crashing up and down. To maintain a general direction into the waves you will need to zig-zag, adding to your distance travelled but it is likely you can maintain a higher speed to compensate.

## Rules of the Road

Road users have the Highway Code to prevent vehicles bumping into each other. On the sea, there are similar rules called, strangely, "Rules of the Road". The full Rules covering all types of vessel are somewhat lengthy and expressed in legal terminology, so for the purposes of small boat users I will summarise the relevant rules here. As there are no roads or white lines, most of the rules concern collision avoidance by making sure everyone understands who gives way to who.

As a general rule, covering all situations, make sure the vessel you are avoiding knows what you are doing by making your own movements obvious. Do not make gentle turns just enough to avoid the other vessel – that could cause them to think you have not altered course and they may make an unpredictable move as a result. Make your turns obvious enough to be recognised, so everyone knows your intentions.

1. Don't expect much larger vessels to treat your small boat as an equal. There are rules that allow them right of way where their movements may be restricted by their draft and the depth of water, and in any case a large vessel under way physically cannot manoeuvre as nimbly as a small boat. Keep well out of their way, you can easily see them coming and in any case they are likely to create a large wash, particularly close to the vessel.

2. Power vessels give way to vessels under sail.

3. All vessels must maintain a safe speed when navigating past other vessels

4. All vessels must maintain a good lookout for other vessels

The following rules assume two power vessels, or sailing vessels under power, are involved.

5. Head to Head: if two vessels are approaching head to head, both vessels alter course to starboard so they pass port to port. Note this is the opposite of what you do on UK roads.

6. When proceeding up a narrow channel or entering harbour, keep to the starboard side in anticipation of vessels coming the other way.

7. If vessels are approaching each other at an angle and likely to collide, the vessel with the other vessel on her starboard side must give way by turning to starboard, which means the vessels pass port side to port side (the same as if they had met head to head).

8. Overtaking vessels must keep clear of vessels they are overtaking.

The International Rules of the Road are available on the web in full – they also cover lights, sound signals, and action in times of low visibility. Just search for "Rules of the Road" – for example the US Coast Guard Navigation Centre has a good site.

---

Tip:

If a vessel is approaching at an angle, you may wonder whether it will pass clear or not. An easy way to check is to watch the bearing between the two boats. If the other vessel appears to be in the same place on your windscreen for a while, it is on the same bearing and you are on a collision course. This method works regardless of angle or speed. If the other vessel is moving across your windscreen in any direction, you will not collide as long as both vessels maintain speed and course.

## Navigation Lights

There are many rules covering different types of vessel under way, working and anchored at night. If you travel at night in busy shipping areas or among working craft, you need to familiarise yourself with the full light recognition system, and you can buy useful recognition cards at good yacht chandlers. The following lights cover the type of small craft and pleasure vessels you are most likely to come across. Larger ships tend to be fairly obvious because of all the other lights showing from working lamps, deck lights and portholes.

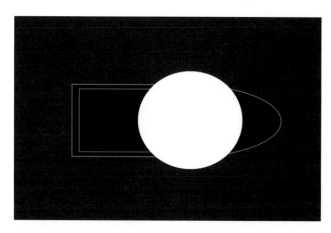

### Under 7 metres in length:
Power driven craft less than 7 metres in length with a maximum speed of 7 knots may show a single white light visible all round.

Vessels at anchor also show a single white light visible all round.

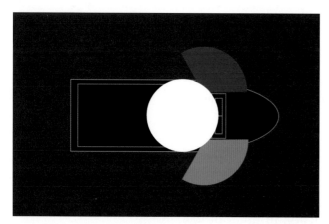

### Under 12 metres in length:
Power driven vessels up to 12 metres in length must show a red port light and a green starboard light, each showing in an arc of 112.5° from the centre line. These lights can be combined into a single unit on the bows or mast, or mounted one on each side of the vessel. A single white light must be visible all round. This is a useful configuration as the single white light can also be used as an anchor light if it is wired and switched separately.

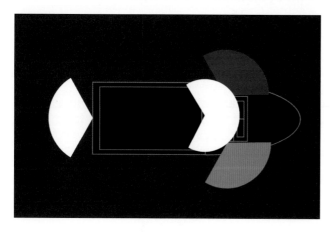

### Under 20 metres in length:
Power driven vessels up to 20 metres in length must show a separate white masthead light facing forward over an arc of 225°, and a white stern light visible over an arc of 135°.

### Sailing Vessels:

Vessels under sail must show the same lights as a power driven vessel under 20 metres in length with the exception of the masthead light. If a sailing vessel is under power it must display the equivalent lights for a power vessel.

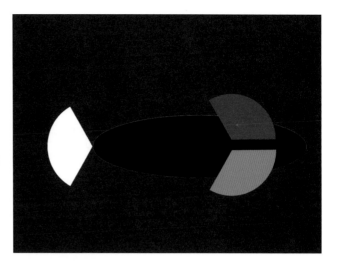

### Vessels over 50 metres in length:

Large vessels under power over 50 metres in length must show two white forward facing masthead lights, a higher one towards the middle or stern, and a lower one towards the bows

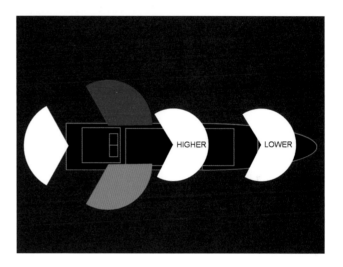

# Man Overboard and Picking Up

Losing someone over the side is nearly as frightening as falling over the side yourself, and it is absolutely essential that the person is picked up from the water as quickly as possible, even in warm weather, as shock and hypothermia can quickly set in. Knowing what to do in these circumstances can save a life, and it is well worth practicing recovering something thrown over the side. The same techniques can be applied to recovering anything, even a much loved hat blown overboard!

If you are cruising along and suddenly you lose something or someone, it is tempting to try and stop and reverse back – in fact this is not what you should do. If you were travelling at speed you could swamp, lose control, or waste valuable time. If you have lost a person, the first thing to do is to throw something floating, preferably a lifebelt, into the water to both mark the position and to provide some assistance to the casualty.

Instead of attempting to stop, you need to quickly and safely turn and travel back up the same track as you were on when the accident happened. This is not a "U" turn, which would put you on a parallel track away from the item or person to be picked up. The manoeuvre to follow is known as the Williamson Turn, which follows a track like a "P" and puts you back on the same track that you were originally travelling on. To do this turn, it is useful to know which is your tightest turning circle (see section Boat Handling – Under Way, explaining propeller torque).

As soon as you know you need to turn, reduce speed and turn 60° in your tightest turn direction, then as soon as the heading has reached 60° from the original heading, immediately turn the wheel in the opposite direction. As the boat will have slowed during these turns, the second turn, although it is against the torque direction, it will still be quite tight as the propeller speed will have reduced. This manoeuvre follows a tight "P" and takes you right back to the casualty.

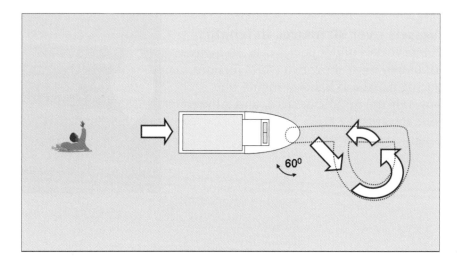

**Williamson Turn**

It is a good idea to practice this with a couple of fenders tied to a bucket thrown over the side. The fenders will be visible, and the bucket will act as a sea-anchor and keep the fenders from being blown around.

Once you have come back to the casualty or object in the water, you need to get it into the boat, and this is surprisingly difficult. As you get close, objects in the water can disappear from the helmsman's view as the line of sight is obstructed by the bows, so it is easy to run past or even run over the object unless a helper keeps watch and provides directions from a different vantage point. Before coming alongside the object, take account of the wind direction and position the boat so it will not drift over the object as soon as the engine is put in neutral. If it is a person in the water and the boat is very light, this can be highly dangerous – again, get to know your boat and how it behaves in these circumstances before you have to do this sort of thing for real.

Getting a waterlogged person back on board, particularly an adult who may by now be weak or in shock, can be very tricky. If you have a bathing platform, try and roll them onto this first. If you have a boarding ladder that extends well into the water, you may be able to help the person on board that way. Rescue craft use a sheet of strong web mesh attached on one side to the gunwhales, with the other side stiffened with a pole and attached with ropes to form a sort of loose cradle. The net is lowered into the water and the casualty can be "floated" into the cradle. The casualty is then lifted by pulling the ropes attached to the opposite side of the cradle, and rolled into the boat. This technique is not easy, even with a trained crew and a low RIB rescue craft.

In the absence of a recovery cradle, which you are unlikely to have to hand, make a loop of rope and pass it to the casualty and get them to slip it over their head and under their arms like a sling. As soon as they have done that, cross the ropes – this gives them a sense of security and something to hang on to. Another loop of rope lowered into the water can act as a step, or they may be able to use the outboard or out-drive leg as a step, but make absolutely sure the engine is out of gear and preferably stopped. You will now have a race against shock and hypothermia on your hands – it is therefore much better to take every precaution against falling over the side in the first place.

## Staying Safely on Board

When under way in a small open boat, waves or unexpected wash can cause sudden changes in direction, particularly if the boat is fast and light. If the helmsman or passengers are not holding on or the movement is particularly violent, they can be thrown against the side of the boat or even flipped out completely. It is very advisable for all crew members to have lifelines and use them. Lifejackets can be purchased with integral harnesses, which have a large stainless steel D ring on the front. Webbing life lines can be purchased with strong snap hooks at each end. One end should always be connected to the D ring, the other can be attached to any strong part of the boat that is convenient. Even if you are thrown about by the sudden motion, at least you will still be in the boat.

If the helmsman is thrown out of his seat it is important that the boat stops rather than continuing at speed with nobody in control. Most petrol engined boats are supplied with a "kill cord" which is a switch attached to a cord, usually red, which has a strap or loop to attach to the helmsman. If the helmsman is thrown from his seat, the cord trips the switch and the engine cuts. Although this prevents a boat from running out of control, the sudden deceleration from high speed will throw everyone forwards. The following wake will catch up with the stern and can force water up into the engine and over the stern into the cockpit, so it is not a situation that can be taken lightly. Take care at all times, as even safety precautions can have secondary dangers for the unwary.

# Fishing Marks

You have your boat, it is in the water, you know how to handle it –
now you want to fish! But unlike rivers and lakes where clues to
fish-holding spots are often very visible, in the sea that is rarely the
case. Looking out from a beach or harbour, you see an expanse of
blue with not a feature on it, but under the surface there are
hundreds of square metres of barren sea-bed, and other spots where
feeding fish are concentrated. So how do you find them?

This is a book about boats, not about angling so I am assuming you
know what species you are looking for, their feeding habits and the
type of underwater structure they like to make their home. The
challenge you now have is relating the type of sea-bed features that
your target fish are likely to inhabit, with the big expanse of blue in
front of you. Where do you start?

**Sources of Information**

First of all, you need to decide what to look for. If you are after wreck
and reef fish such as pollack and conger, you need to find the
location of a wreck or an area where rocks extend above the sea-bed.
If you are after fish that frequent fast-moving water over sand-banks
such as bass and turbot, you will need to find areas of smooth
undulating bottom in a good tide run. If you are after general
bottom fishing, then finding holes, gullies, broken rocks or banks in
areas of otherwise smooth bottom will tend to concentrate fish. Fish
need to eat, breed and survive and as they are in evolutionary terms
not very advanced creatures, they have little time for much else. So
the ground they inhabit must provide food, shelter from predators
or a place to spawn and those basic drivers will dictate which fish
turn up where.

One option is to motor about on the sea looking at your fish-finder
until something interesting appears on the screen. Don't discount
this method, as this may be a way of finding that secret mark
nobody else knows about, but it is probably not the most
productive way to start.

One of the best sources of information is from other anglers that
you meet in local angling shops, angling clubs or around launch
sites and marinas. Making friends, sharing information, being
prepared to give as much as take, respecting other's privacy and not
being too pushy will mean that sooner or later you will be pointed
in the right direction. You may not be given specific coordinates for
a mark, but you may be able to pick up tips about general areas
within which you can explore and find your own marks.

Your large scale Admiralty charts will be vital in your search for marks. Yachting charts have little detail of the bottom, but Admiralty charts are created for commercial users and contain a great deal of information about the undulations of the bottom, the location of wrecks, and what are referred to as "obstructions". These latter features are shown on charts so trawlers can avoid them, and they are usually well scattered areas of wreck or some unknown object that has been reported by a commercial fisherman. A study of the chart will show banks, gullies, holes and wrecks – which is exactly what you are looking for. Unfortunately it does not tell you which ones hold the most fish, so you will have to combine this information with some other research – which may include going out there and having a look.

Reefs are more difficult to find as they are not specifically marked. However, if you cast your mind back to your school geography lessons you can spot some clues on the land. Hills and reefs have something in common – they are often formed in the same way. They can be areas of harder rock that have eroded more slowly than the surrounding landscape, or they could have been formed by the "folding" of the layers of rock as the Earth's crust moved over millions of years. The rock that forms the seaside landscape is usually the same as the rock under the sea at that point, and an area of hill running down to the sea could extend under the sea in the form of an area of reef. It may not, of course, but it is worth checking.

Another very useful source of information on the location and description of wrecks and well-populated reefs are books and web sites created by, and for scuba divers. As divers like to share information (unlike anglers who fear commercial fishermen raiding the marks), the wreck locations are freely available and there are usually very good descriptions of the size and state of the wreck, orientation and accessibility. If you arrive at a mark and find divers present, move on to another mark and come back when they have finished. Dives do not last very long, and take place when tides are slack – which is usually a poor time for fishing, so give them some space in return for the information you have borrowed.

You may be lucky enough to come across a book with a guide to fishing in your area, with some indication of good marks. Sea angling magazines also have regional guides from time to time, so it is worth keeping an eye on the newsagent's shelves for useful issues. The final source of information on marks needs a bit of careful handling – other boats fishing. Anglers, and particularly charter boat skippers, can be very possessive about their marks although there are no ownership rights on any particular piece of seabed. A good mark is often shown up by a number of boats fishing in close proximity, and if you come up slowly and fish nearby without crowding other boats, it is unlikely anyone will mind. Where boats are well spread out, it probably means this is a good general fishing area – you can check the bottom with your fish-finder. If they are in a line, they may be fishing a bank – in which case go to the end of the line or fish in a gap between boats.

If you see a single boat fishing, this may be someone who has a special mark, or an idiot who doesn't know what he is doing. It is hard to tell the difference from a distance, so in case it is the former, you need to be somewhat diplomatic in your approach. One way to infuriate a professional charter skipper is to approach his boat closely, press the "Mark" button on your GPS, and fish away, or return later. There is nothing he can do about it, but it won't make you popular and you don't want to make enemies in the small world of boat angling. However, there is a way of using another boats position to find a good mark. If you see a boat fishing, pass well clear but mark the position on your GPS and make a note of the other boat's position relative to your own at that point. It might be 200 metres North of where you marked the position. When you return later to the marked position, travel 200 metres North and you will be where the other boat was fishing. You can then motor around slowly checking the fish-finder to see if there was a particular sea-bed feature that was the mark.

However you find your fishing marks, the location is not the only piece of information you need. Some marks fish better at different stages of the tide, at different seasons of the year, or for different species. You can only gain that information from someone who is prepared to share it with you, or by trying your marks at different times, different dates and with different methods.

Your first year of fishing will involve a lot of learning and probably not a great deal of catching. But take courage, as what you have learned will help you fish better next year, and next year, and the next year. Keep a careful record of where you fished, tide, date, weather, fish caught and other observations – it will form a very useful record to look back on in future years. There is a catch record template included in the Appendices of this book.

# Tides

Most of us learned a little about tides at school, and what we learned suddenly becomes very relevant when we go to sea. If you were a beach angler, or even just a holidaymaker, you will have been familiar with the ebb and flow of the tides as they come in and go out. Less obvious to those on land is the fact that the water does not just go up and down, it flows around the coast and creates currents which change direction and speed as well as causing the sea level to rise and fall. There are usually two high tides each day, and the tide times advance each day which is why you need to refer to tide tables to find out the times of high and low water on specific days.

The movement of a large body of water on the Earth's surface is caused by the gravitational pull of the Moon. High tide occurs when the position on the Earth's surface is nearest the moon. The Moon takes 28 days to go round the earth, so in one revolution of the earth the moon has moved on by one twenty-eighth of a day and the original point has to move a further twenty-eighth of a revolution to be closest to the moon again. One twenty-eighth of 24 hours is 51.4 minutes, which means that in theory, high tide is 51.4 minutes later each day. There are a number of terrestrial factors which modify this theoretical period between high tides, so tide tables will not always show an exact 51 minutes difference from day to day, but it will be close enough as a general rule. This means the time of high water advances approximately one hour each day.

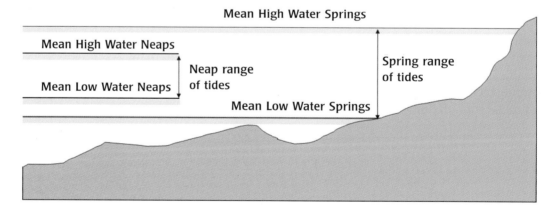

The tidal range is the vertical distance between high water and low water. A neap tide is a tide with a narrow range, which is a low high water and a high low water. A spring tide is the opposite, with a high, high water and a low, low water, resulting in a large tidal range. Heights of tides are important for navigation and angling, because the tide range may determine whether you can navigate a shallow channel at low tide, and the tidal strength will affect the behaviour and location of fish.

Tides vary in height and strength of current according to the lunar calendar, and the pattern is generally cyclical with the tidal range increasing daily until a there are a series of spring tides, then reducing daily until neaps are reached. Tide times are published in tide tables, which can be purchased cheaply in angling shops and chandlers, or are available in local newspapers or on the web.

A good table will also show heights as well as times of high and low tides. Tide times are different for each point around the coast, because the tide "flows" along the shore and high water will occur at different times in different locations. These tidal differences are constant, so for example high water at Langstone Harbour will always be the same number of minutes earlier than high water Portsmouth, regardless of the time of the tide. These tidal differences are published in Almanacs and tide tables, and to obtain the exact time of tides for your chosen place, you will have to refer to the tide table of the nearest published port and make an adjustment based on the published differences.

---

Tip:

You will notice that spring tides tend to coincide with high water at the same time in a particular location, which makes it easy to predict tidal strength. For example, in Portsmouth, high tides at midday are always higher, or springs; high tides in the early morning and late evening are always lower, or neaps.

---

There are some oddities in tidal behaviour caused by the geography of the land. As the tidal currents move towards Britain, the flow divides around the land and runs down the coast on the east side and the west. The currents meet along the south coast, but because the coast of Britain is not symmetrical, the high tide times do not exactly meet at the same time. This results in the phenomenon of a double high water or a high water stand such as those around Christchurch and Southampton.

Other tidal irregularities are less easy to predict and are caused by the weather. A prolonged onshore wind can "push" the water and increase the height of the tide. Atmospheric pressure variations can also play a part. This means the time and heights of high and low water in published tables can be significantly different from reality, varying from a few minutes up to a hour and more.

# Weather Forecasts

The weather can make the difference between a safe enjoyable day out and a frightening, dangerous and uncomfortable experience. The weather can change faster than a small boat as sea can return to the safety of harbour, so it is essential that you know what the weather conditions are at sea before you set out, and how the weather is expected to change while you are out there.

If you were not taught about the weather at school, or have forgotten the significant details, there are many books on the subject and some excellent resources on-line. The UK Meteorological Office has a learning resource centre for different ability levels and much of the information available is centred around understanding the day to day weather changes, and how to interpret forecasts and weather charts. This is exactly what is needed to be able to plan a safe trip to sea in a small boat.

The most important weather element to predict is the wind strength and direction. The second most important is visibility – both affect your safety at sea. Other factors like sunshine, temperature and rain will affect your comfort levels and therefore need to be anticipated so you can prepare accordingly and still enjoy your day.

The United Kingdom has notoriously changeable weather, and this is caused by its position on Earth. There are competing influences on the country, from cool air from the north, warm air from the south, wet air from the west and dry air from the east. The prevailing or most common air stream is warm damp air from the south west. At any time, one influence can become more dominant and deflect the other air streams away, which means long term forecasts are rarely accurate.

Despite huge advances in the understanding of weather and the technology for capturing and analysing information, even short term forecasts are not completely accurate so before any trip you need to keep an eye on the developing weather trends, read the latest forecasts before you set out, and keep an eye on the weather while you are fishing. If you have any concerns about the weather, don't take chances – stay close to shore so if the weather deteriorates you can quickly reach shelter and safety.

Most weather forecasts are provided for people based on land, so there tends to be more predictions of sunshine or rain. Less attention is paid to wind strength and direction unless it is very strong, so for the level of detail the boat owner needs a more specialist weather forecast is required.

The UK Meteorological Office provides two forecasts for boat operators: firstly the Shipping Forecast, updated twice a day covering large areas of sea up to hundreds of miles across, from Spain to Iceland. A second forecast, of more relevance to boat anglers, is the Inshore Waters Forecast, again issued twice a day covering areas up to twelve miles from the coast. In addition there are reports from coastal stations of the actual conditions at the time. Both are available from the Met Office web site or by premium rate phone services. The Shipping Forecast is also broadcast on BBC Radio 4 Long Wave.

The Shipping Forecast is announced in a structured manner and needs interpretation to understand what is meant. Each area of sea described has a name, and each area is described separately or several areas may be grouped together. There is a map of these areas on the Met Office web site.

At the start of the announcement there will be warnings of any gale force winds (Beaufort Scale Force 8 or above) that are in force or imminent. The announcer will describe the general trends, then expected weather for each area as follows:

------------------------------------------------------------------------

"THIS IS THE SHIPPING FORECAST ISSUED BY THE MET OFFICE, ON BEHALF OF THE MARITIME AND COASTGUARD AGENCY, AT 1725 ON FRIDAY 07 OCTOBER 2005

THERE ARE WARNINGS OF GALES IN VIKING NORTH UTSIRE SOUTH UTSIRE MALIN HEBRIDES BAILEY FAIR ISLE FAEROES AND SOUTHEAST ICELAND

THE GENERAL SYNOPSIS AT 1300
FRONTAL TROUGH FAEROES TO SHANNON EXPECTED VIKING TO FITZROY BY 1300 TOMORROW. RIDGE OF HIGH PRESSURE FISHER TO BISCAY GRADUALLY DECLINING

THE AREA FORECASTS FOR THE NEXT 24 HOURS

VIKING NORTH UTSIRE SOUTH UTSIRE
SOUTH OR SOUTHEAST 7 OR GALE 8, OCCASIONALLY SEVERE GALE 9 IN VIKING AND NORTH UTSIRE FOR A TIME, VEERING WEST 4 IN VIKING LATER. RAIN LATER. MODERATE OR POOR…….." etc.

------------------------------------------------------------------------

This might sound like a code, but it is fairly easy to interpret.

# Shipping Forecast

**Wind Speeds** are given according to the Beaufort Scale (see table in the Appendices)

**Wind Direction** refers to the direction the wind is blowing from.

**Veering** means a changing to the direction of the wind clockwise, e.g. South to West.

**Backing** means a changing to the direction of the wind anticlockwise, e.g. South to East.

**Imminent** means in the next six hours

**Soon** means in the next six to twelve hours

**Later** means after twelve hours

The final description in each area refers to visibility, as follows:

**Fog** – Visibility less than 1,000 metres

**Poor** – Visibility between 1,000 metres and 2 nautical miles

**Moderate** – Visibility between 2 and 5 nautical miles

**Good** – Visibility more than 5 nautical miles

A more detailed glossary is provided on the Met Office web site.

## Inshore Waters Forecast

The Inshore Waters Forecast is also divided up into areas, this time according to parts of the coast between specific landmarks. The weather description is less cryptic than the Shipping Forecast, and includes the Sea State which is of great interest to anglers who plan to spend hours at anchor. An example follows:

---

**Issued by the Met Office at 1700 UTC on Friday 07 October.**

**Inshore Waters Forecast to 12 miles offshore from 1700 UTC to 1700 UTC.**

**From Cape Wrath to Rattray Head including Orkney.**

24 hour forecast:
**Wind:** south 5 to 7, occasionally gale 8 in north at first, veering southwest 4 or 5, increasing 6 in west later.
**Weather:** rain spreading from west, then showers later.
**Visibility:** moderate or poor becoming good.
**Sea State:** moderate or rough.
**Outlook for the following 24 hours:**
**Wind:** southwest 5 or 6 backing south 6 to gale 8, perhaps severe gale 9 in north later.
**Weather:** showers then rain.
**Visibility:** good becoming moderate.
**Sea State:** moderate building rough.

After the full UK coastline is covered, there is a general long term forecast, such as:

**Outlook for all UK Inshore Waters for following 3 days:**
Gale or severe gale southwest winds off west and north Scotland moving away on Sunday night with strong southerly winds elsewhere moderating on Monday. Fresh or strong southerly winds during Tuesday and Wednesday.

---

Even if you have no knowledge or interest in the weather, you are obliged by SOLAS V regulations to check the weather forecasts before a trip  and get regular updates if you are out for any length of time. Checking and understanding the Met Office Inshore Waters and Shipping Forecast is the very minimum you should do.

> Tip:
>
> Do a web search for local web-cams and weather stations to get up to the minute weather statistics over the web. For example, Hayling Island has a web cam pointing at the shore at **www.hayling.co.uk/surfcam**. There is a weather station transmitting live weather and sea state statistics from the approaches to Chichester Harbour entrance at **www.chimet.co.uk**

# Basic Navigation

## Understanding Charts

Charts are essential for any fishing trip – they are your map of the sea for guiding you out and back, without which you might feel overwhelmed by the expanse of grey-green around you! Charts also show useful fishing marks such as underwater obstructions and wrecks; banks, hollows, overfalls and other fishy areas.

The only charts worth considering for anglers are the detailed Admiralty charts published by the UK Hydrographic Office. There are "Small Boat" Leisure editions which are smaller and have less detail, but are quite handy to have in the boat. Portfolio Editions are several charts of an area, printed on the same size paper and supplied in a plastic pouch. Don't be tempted by charts from other publishers, these are usually for yachtsmen, not anglers, and although they are perfectly adequate for navigation they do not carry enough sea-bed information for our needs.

Charts quickly go out of date as buoys are moved or the sea-bed re-surveyed. These changes are published as "Notices to Mariners" on the UKHO web site so you can annotate your charts with the updated information, or you can take your charts to an authorised distributor of charts to be updated for a fee.

Charts can be supplied flat or folded, and will look like any other map, except that the area with all the detail is the sea, and the area with very little detail is the land. There are usually useful notes dotted around in areas of land, or on the back. There will also be several 360° compass graduations showing true north (always at the top) and magnetic variation.

There are graduations marked along the top and bottom of the chart which are the degrees of longitude, and graduations marked along both sides which are the points of latitude. One minute of latitude is always equal to one nautical mile – that saves you looking for a scale.

Refer to the chart key to understand the symbols – with Admiralty charts this is supplied in a separate booklet. Some are self explanatory, like "Wk" indicating a wreck. Some are more mystifying, such as a buoy with a name and something like "Fl(2)G.10s" which in fact describes the light flashing sequence for that particular buoy at night.

Depths are marked in three ways: by colour, by lines, which are like above-water contour lines only in reverse, and by numbers. Areas covered at high water and exposed at low water are also shown, with the drying height shown as a number with a line under it. The

"Charted Depth" is the depth at the lowest point of the lowest tide – you need to allow for the additional depth of water if the tide is at any other stage.

Dotted around the sea you will also see letters in diamonds – purple in the case of Admiralty Leisure Editions. These will refer to a table somewhere else on the chart, and show the speed and direction of tidal flow at that point on the chart, at high water, and for each hour of the six hours before and six hours after.

Even if you have a chart-plotter with electronic charts, I strongly recommend you carry paper charts as well. These are essential if your plotter fails, and are also useful for planning at home, and to give a wider view of your fishing area than you can see on a tiny screen.

The sea does not have clearly marked routes like roads on land, nor are all dangers visible on the surface. Various marks are put in or on the sea to indicate safe areas and danger areas. At one time there were many different systems around the World, so in 1979, a body called the International Association of Lighthouse Authorities (IALA) was formed to unify the different buoyage systems in use. They were nearly successful, as we now have two similar systems, IALA 'A' used in the UK and Europe; and IALA 'B' used in North and South America, Japan and the Philippines. This section will concentrate on the European IALA 'A' system.

Do not tie up to a buoy in order to fish – it is illegal and highly dangerous, both to yourself and for others who depend on a clear sight of the buoy for safe navigation.

Buoys and marks are an invaluable navigational asset, but their presence or absence from their expected place cannot be guaranteed. Anchored buoys can drag their moorings in a storm, be sunk in a collision with a large ship, or be removed for maintenance. You are always advised to check with some other indicator as well, such as your depth on the fish-finder or bearings from a fixed landmark.

# Buoys and Marks

**Lateral Marks**

On leaving your launch site or marina for the very first time, it is highly likely that buoys or posts called Lateral Marks are the first navigation objects you will see. These are used to mark the navigable channel, and are aligned in the 'A' system to be on the Port or Starboard hand as you are approaching a port. The historical reason for this was because for a vessel making for a safe harbour in heavy weather, it was one less thing to worry about – the red markers would always be left to port and green to starboard. On leaving the port after a storm, it would be less stressful so the helmsman would have time to work out that red on the port side coming in meant leave red on the starboard side when going out, and that is how you use the Lateral Marks in the UK today.

Lateral Marks may be buoys or posts. The distinguishing features are that the port hand marks are red in colour and are square or have a square shape on top; starboard hand marks are conical or have a conical mark on top. The shape is important, as a buoy in poor repair, or covered in weed or bird droppings may not be easily identifiable by colour but it will have a distinctively different shape.

At night they may have lights as well – red for port and green for starboard. The sequence of flashes (referred to as rhythm) will vary and will be identified on the relevant chart.

Some objects that could be hazardous to shipping are marked with a buoy or post with black and red bands, and two black balls on top. This could be a wreck or rock that lies just below the surface. Not all dangerous areas are marked in this way, usually only those very close to regularly used shipping channels. Keep well clear of these marks, but unless there are other marks you can pass on any side.

Conversely, areas of safe water not otherwise marked as channels are indicated with posts or buoys coloured with red and white vertical bands, with a red ball on top.

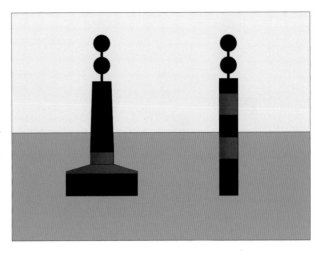

**Isolated Danger Marks**

Tip:

Buoys are not always what they seem. The stripes on posts can be misleading if seen at low tide where a large, dark section is exposed. Cormorants sitting on top of a post will make the top mark appear different. Bird guano will obscure the colour of poorly maintained marks. Take a good look just to make sure.

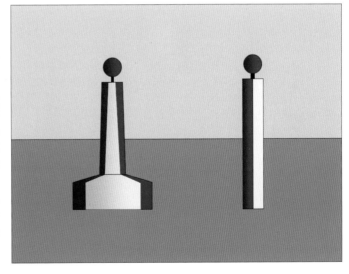

Another common buoy or mark, usually found close to a busy harbour or estuary, are the "special" marks. These are always yellow, and could mean many things, but they are not of navigational significance. They could be temporary, indicating a turning point for a yacht race, they could mark the position of a regularly dived wreck, or they could be where they are for a host of other reasons. Sometimes they are marked on the charts, but not always.

**Safe Water Marks**

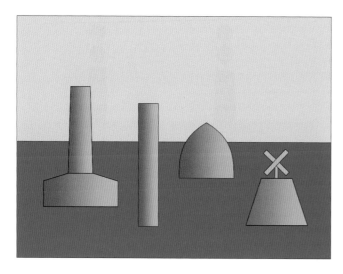

**Special Marks**

One of the most important sets of marks to learn, and in some respects these are probably the most complicated, are the Cardinal Marks. These may appear singly, in pairs, or all four and show the position of a point of danger relative to the buoy, that is, the danger zone will be North, South, East or West of the buoy depending on the colour sequence and orientation of the triangular top marks. The diagram below shows where the danger area is relative to each type of Cardinal Mark.

For example, if you are travelling from East to West and you see a buoy in front of you coloured black on top and yellow below, with two triangles on top each pointing upwards, this would be a North Cardinal Mark indicating a danger zone to the South of it. In this case you would alter course to starboard to go to the North of the North Cardinal Mark and stay well clear of the danger. Always check other marks around and make sure by avoiding one danger you are not putting yourself into another.

**Cardinal Marks**

If you are heading out from the harbour, and heading for a fishing mark you have been told of of, you have probably already come across the terms Latitude and Longitude. However, there is a little more to it than was covered in your school geography lessons, so we will go over the basics and the important parts that relate to coastal navigation.

# Latitude and Longitude

## Latitude

Your position north or south of the equator is expressed in degrees of latitude, with the equator as zero degrees latitude. Positions above the equator are referred to as degrees north and positions below the equator are known as degrees south. Lines of latitude are equally spaced, and one degree of latitude is always 60 nautical miles at any point on the globe.

## Longitude

A line drawn from the north pole to the south pole through Greenwich is the line of zero degrees longitude, or The Prime Meridian. Positions to the east of it are expressed as degrees east and positions west of it are degrees west. Lines of longitude radiate from the north and south poles, so the distance between them is widest at the equator and get closer together the further north or south you go. One degree of longitude is therefore not a constant distance.

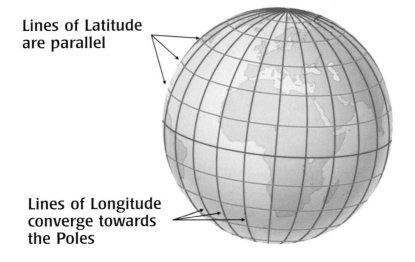

**Lines of Latitude are parallel**

**Lines of Longitude converge towards the Poles**

## Describing a position in latitude and longitude

One degree of latitude or longitude is divided into 60 minutes, and one minute of latitude or longitude is divided into 60 seconds. These are mathematical seconds and have nothing to do with time.

There are several different ways of expressing a position, but the convention used for maritime navigation – and most importantly, the position you would describe to the coastguard in the event of an emergency, is in degrees, minutes and decimal minutes. For example, the wreck of the tug Blazer lies off the Scilly Isles in the position:

### 49° 45' 330N  06° 19' 400W

When describing this position, you would say:

**"Forty nine degrees, forty five decimal three three zero minutes north; zero six degrees nineteen decimal four zero zero minutes west."**

You can see that if one degree of latitude is 60 nautical miles, with 60 minutes to a degree and three decimal places, the position described in that way would be accurate to plus or minus 1.85 metres!

## Chart Datums

Historically, different countries have used different points of reference to map lines of latitude and longitude, which means the position described above could only be found if you knew which reference point, or datum, the position was relative to. In the UK most maps and charts are in Ordnance Survey (OS) datum and in order to match your GPS unit to OS maps you would have to set it to OS datum. In order to rationalise these different datums, a world geodetic survey was published in 1984 and it is now possible to produce maps and charts of the earth's surface to one common datum, called WGS84. Many countries are in the process of converting their country's maps and charts to WGS84 datum, and the UK Admiralty are converting UK maritime charts from the OS datum. At the time of writing there is an interim situation where some charts and maps are still in local datums and some in the WGS84 datum.

It is therefore essential to know which datum your paper charts and GPS unit are using, because confusing the two could make a difference of several hundred metres – enough to put you well clear of the fishing mark you are looking for, or worse, you could track right into a rock or sandbank that you thought you had positioned yourself well clear of. As long as you know the datum your position is taken from, and you set that datum when you enter the position on your GPS, when you change the datum setting on your GPS it will automatically convert stored positions to the required datum. There are also web sites that have datum conversion tools if you are planning your trip away from your GPS unit.

## Your compass and north

True north is at the top of your chart, and is the most northerly point on the earth's surface. Magnetic north is not exactly true north, and to complicate matters, it is constantly moving and is different in different parts of the world. The difference between magnetic north and true north is called Magnetic Variation. Your chart will indicate the magnetic variation for the area in question, and you will have to adjust that figure for the difference between the date the variation figure was given and the current date.

If that doesn't sound complicated enough, there is another factor that affects where your magnetic compass will point. That is the influence other metallic objects in your boat will have on the magnetic compass. The difference can be considerable, and is likely to be different depending on which direction your boat is heading. This is called Magnetic Deviation.

Each boat will have a different magnetic deviation because the metallic objects on a boat are likely to be placed differently. This means you will need to know the magnetic deviation for each course direction. Working this out is called "swinging the compass". Electronic compasses also suffer from deviation as they have a magnetic sender unit, but their electronic wizardry makes swinging the compass easy, and the compensation for deviation is applied automatically.

Swinging a traditional compass is more tedious, and involves heading in known directions on all major points of the compass – at least eight, and recording the difference between the known direction and the course indicated on the compass. These differences are then plotted graphically, and a smooth line drawn joining up these points so the deviation on courses in between those you have plotted can be estimated reasonably accurately. This magnetic variation reference card is an important asset in traditional chart-based navigation.

With the widespread use of GPS for navigation, it would be very easy to dismiss all of this and just punch in the destination and press the "Go To" button, and the unit will display the bearing and your course. As long as these two are kept nearly the same you will get there. However, navigating a long distance, a complex course along the coast, or getting home after your GPS has failed will involve traditional navigational skills where an understanding of your compass, variation and deviation will be essential.

# Compasses, Courses and Bearings

There are three purposes of a compass on board a small boat: to show orientation, or which way your boat is pointing; to show the direction of the course you are taking (which may not be the same thing); and to indicate the bearing or direction, of an object from your boat.

To provide this information, there are three type of compass that you may have on board. The minimum you must have for any form of navigation is the steering compass. This is fitted permanently to the boat, oriented so that there is a fixed line on the glass to show the direction your boat is heading and is used to steer a course. These compasses can be traditional magnetic card types, with a rotating, graduated card in some form of dampening liquid, or an electronic compass with a digital display fed from a remote directional sensor.

You may also have a hand-bearing compass. This is designed to read bearings from a remote landmark by aligning sights, much like a rifle, on the mark and reading off the bearing. Again, these can be rotating cards or electronic. The third type of compass is not really a compass at all, but as your GPS will display your most recent course track in terms of a heading, it can be included here. In addition, your GPS will provide a bearing from your present position to the destination waypoint, and will also show the track from the origin of the course to the destination.

It is important to understand the difference between the boat's heading and the boat's course or track, particularly if you are using both a GPS and a steering compass. The GPS will take no account of the movement of water – at all times, it is fixing positions based on the absolute position relative to the sea-bed, or what is called "over the ground". The course or track that is displayed is calculated by the GPS by comparing the previous position with the current position. If the boat is drifting with no power, swinging around with the wind, the track of the boat over the ground will be displayed as a course, regardless of which direction the boat is heading.

Similarly, if the boat is kept on a constant heading according to the steering compass, but wind or tide is exerting a significant sideways force, the actual course over the ground will not be the same as the heading, as the boat will tend to "crab" at an angle to the heading, according to the strength of wind or tide. The significance of this effect will depend on the distance you are travelling, the speed of the boat and strength of wind and tide. For most small, fast boats heading for inshore marks this tends to be ignored. For a slow boat heading for a mid-channel wreck with a strong tide running, it is an important consideration in navigation.

If you have a GPS, it is too tempting to key in your destination, read off the bearing displayed and head for it. I am sure that is exactly how many boat owners navigate, and I am also sure you will too, but don't let that be the only way you navigate. You could have mistyped the coordinates, there could be dangerous shoals or rocks in your path, or your GPS could fail. You need to know the basics of navigation to get the best out of a GPS, and to help you out in case you can't rely on it for any reason. If you have an interest in the subject, evening classes or a short course are very enjoyable and will add to your skills. If you just want the basics, here is a short guide but I strongly recommend you read up on the subject from books readily available from yacht chandlers.

The inside of a small boat at sea is probably the worst possible place to be plotting a course. You need a large flat surface, good light, dryness and no movement to make you feel queasy with prolonged studying. Hardly the description of the inside of a small angling boat! Instead, start your trip early by doing the planning and course plotting at home – it all adds to the fun anyway.

To plan your trip, you will need some very basic tools: a large scale chart or charts covering your planned route, a soft pencil, a soft rubber, and either a set of parallel rules (available from a yacht chandlers), or you can make do with a normal ruler and a set-square. You will also need tidal information for the date of your trip, and preferably a tidal atlas covering the route as well.

# Plotting Your Course

---

Tip:

Paper charts in an open boat, or even one with a cuddy, are vulnerable to water damage. You can buy plastic chart pockets, but these usually fit only the smaller folio-scaled charts. To water-proof a chart, paint it with a water-repellent liquid of the type used to treat brick walls. A small can will cover more charts than you will ever need, and can be bought cheaply from a DIY store.

---

The first task is to adjust the direction of magnetic north on your chart for variation. As described earlier, variation is the difference between magnetic north and true north, and is changing year by year. Your chart will have a date, and the annual change, marked on it, usually in the printed compass rose itself. For example, if your chart date (which is the date printed on it, not the date you bought it) is six years old and the change in variation is 10 minutes per year East, that means reduce the variation by 60 seconds or one degree to align with your boats compass which will be reading the magnetic north of today. If your chart date is recent and the change in variation is small, you can ignore this for short journeys as the difference it makes will be marginal anyway.

Let us assume you want to know what course to steer to get from your launch site to a fishing mark you have been told of, which is approximately five miles out to sea. Firstly, identify your destination by reading off the latitude (along the horizontal scale) and the longitude (along the vertical scale). Using your ruler and setsquare you will be able to mark a pencil cross where the fishing mark is located.

Next, draw a line from your launch site to the mark, and provided that route does not take you into a danger spot like a rock or sandbank, that is your intended track. The angle of that track from magnetic north is the course you would steer if there was no wind and no tide to push you in a different direction. You can find out the course to steer by drawing a line exactly parallel with your course, through the nearest compass rose on the chart. This is where parallel rules come in handy, to "step" a parallel line from your course line to the compass mark.

You now need to take account of wind and tide, which a GPS will not do. Unless the forces of wind and tide are directly in front of or behind you, they will keep pushing you boat off the intended track. Your GPS will keep modifying your intended course to keep you headed towards the destination mark, but your actual course over the ground will not be the planned track. If you do not have a GPS and follow a compass course, you will miss the destination entirely.

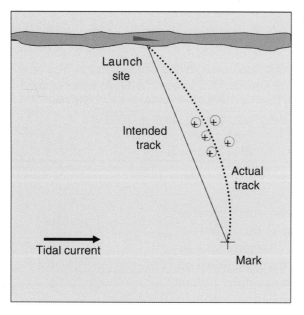

This can be very dangerous if there are rocks just down-tide of your planned course as in the illustration here, because if you follow the exact compass course or the bearings given by the GPS, you will end up right among the rocks instead of on the safe course between the launch site and the mark.

**With GPS**

To allow for tidal drift, you need to calculate the length of time you will be travelling, and the distance and direction you will travel in that time pushed by the tide. The direction and speed of the expected tide at the time you will be travelling can be calculated from tide tables for the date of your trip, together with the table provided on the chart, or from the tidal atlas. The easiest way to calculate the course you need to steer to compensate for the effect of the tide flow is to draw a line on the chart, of a length that is scaled to the chart representing the distance you would drift in the time you are travelling on that course, and the angle of the line is the angle of the tidal current. Draw the line pointing up-tide of the mark, then draw a line joining the "start" end of your line of drift, to the start point of the course. This line is the course you must steer, but the line directly from the start point to the mark is the actual track of your boat. Here is a simple worked example.

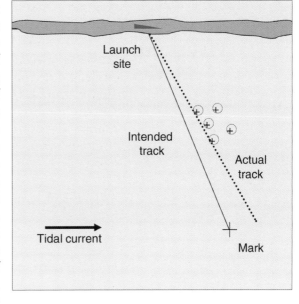

**With Magnetic Compass**

- Your boat travels at 10 knots

- You wish to travel from the launch site to the mark, a distance of five nautical miles.

- Therefore you will be travelling for 30 minutes

- The tide is running at 1 knot from west to east.

- In thirty minutes you will drift half a nautical mile

- You must steer a constant course to point **A**, to end up on your mark at point **B**

- **Remember to adjust the magnetic course calculated with your chart according to the deviation card for your boat's compass on that heading.**

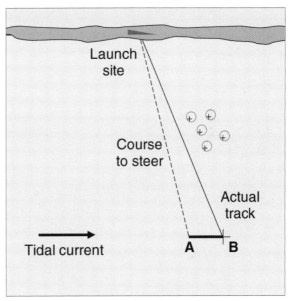

**Allowing for Tidal Current**

Whether you chose to plan every trip like this, or to go on to study coastal navigation in more detail, is up to you. This is only a very basic introduction but it is important that you are at least aware of the effects of wind and tide on courses suggested to you by your GPS. You can then make allowances for drift to ensure you reach your mark safely and do not inadvertently end up in danger.

## Bearings, Fixes and Marks

If all your marks are based on GPS co-ordinates you may never need to worry about taking bearings, but it is worth knowing about in case you are told of a mark based on bearings, or in case you need to describe your position according to bearings in an emergency. Before the days of GPS, taking bearings on distant objects to confirm or "fix" your position was an essential part of navigation. This is a simple description of how it is done.

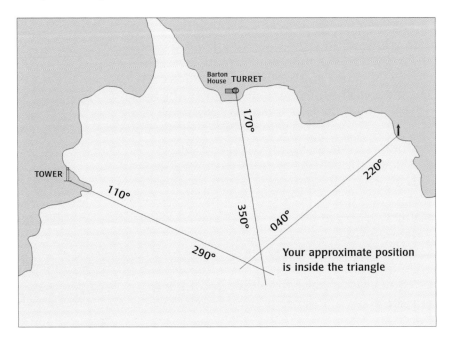

**Bearing Fix**

A hand-bearing compass is used to aim at a fixed object, which has to be one that has a confirmed position on your chart, and the bearing displayed on the compass is recorded. You may need to do this several times and take an average if the boat is moving about. If you draw a line on your chart on the reciprocal angle, i.e. the bearing you recorded plus 180°, your position is somewhere along it. If you do exactly the same with another object, preferably one about 90° to the first one, the point at which these two lines intersect is where you are, in theory.

In practice, because boats wobble about, compasses swing, pencil lines are thick and rulers can slip, it probably is not. To obtain a more accurate fix, you need to take a third bearing of another object and draw a third line. In theory again, this line should go through the intersection of the first two. In practice, it will create a little triangle, and you are somewhere inside of it. If your triangle is fairly small, that is probably good enough. If it is big, you had better start again.

# Anchoring

Most books on sailing and powerboats cover anchoring, but assume that you are anchoring in a sheltered bay for the night. Anchoring for a boat angler is a very different matter – the water will be deeper, the tide will run harder and the anchor has to be set as accurately as possible to ensure you are among the fish.

The job of the anchor is to grip the sea-bed, and not move until you want to. The job of the rope is to connect your boat to the anchor, so the anchor can do its job best. As with most things in a boat, there are plenty of choices which can confuse the beginner.

## Anchor, Rope and Chain

Starting with anchors, there are several different types, with varieties of each type according to manufacturer. Most will be made of steel or cast iron, heavily galvanised to protect against rust. Some super-yachts have stainless steel anchors, and aluminium anchors are available for certain limited conditions, but these are unlikely to be suitable, or affordable, for the boat angler.

Each anchor has advantages and disadvantages, and many anglers swear by one or another. The choice will be dictated by your needs or preference. The weight of anchor to buy can also be a worry, so I would recommend that once you have selected a style of anchor, you ask someone knowledgeable in a yacht chandlers, and tell them the length and weight of your boat and the type of anchoring you intend to do. Anchors are sized by weight, and the only disadvantage of having one heavier than needed is the effort required to raise it. One lighter than it should be may not hold you firmly in position – which is what you need it to do.

Different types of anchor are as follows:

**Fisherman.** This is the "traditional" anchor, used for centuries and still in widespread use. They usually have a folding "stock" which has to be pegged in place to ensure the flukes dig in the seabed. This makes them more cumbersome to use, and the protruding fluke and stock are prone to tangling with the anchor chain. Fisherman anchors will not "self-stow" on a bow roller because of the protruding stock. You need a slightly heavier fisherman anchor to give the same holding power as other styles, which is a consideration when hauling up from a great depth.

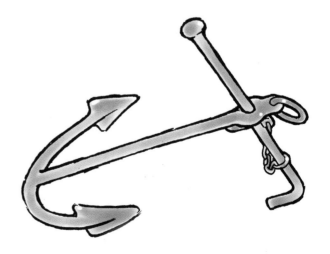

**Fisherman Anchor**

**Danforth Anchor**

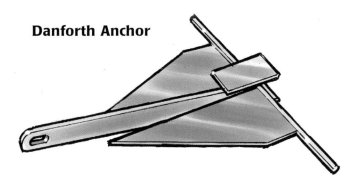

**Danforth.** Good general purpose designs, and fold flat when not in use. Some people think they do not hold as well in some types of sea bed, but in my experience they work as well as any other style. They cannot be rigged to trip with a cord as they are designed to hinge and dig into the seabed from either side. Be careful when handling as fingers can be pinched between the stock and flukes. They can usually be persuaded to self-stow on a bow roller but need additional fastening due to the lack of an "elbow".

**CQR or Plough Anchor**

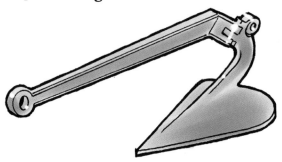

**CQR or Plough.** As the name suggests these have a plough shaped head which may be fixed or hinged. They hold well in most sea beds and also nestle conveniently if you chose to stow you anchor permanently on a bow roller. If you do not, they are less convenient to store in the boat as they do not fold flat.

**Bruce Anchor**

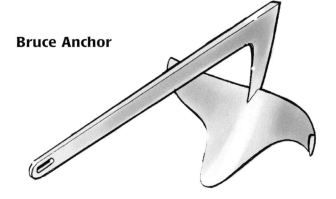

**Bruce.** This is a modern design with exceptional holding power for their weight. Like the plough anchor, unless they are stowed on a bow roller they are not very convenient to store as they do not fold flat.

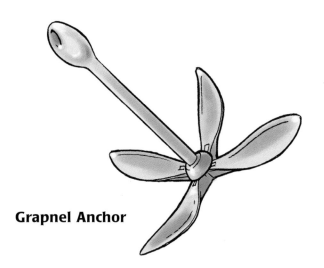

**Grapnel.** These are available in smaller sizes at very low cost but are not as effective as the other styles except for rocky areas. Shop-bought ones have folding flukes which make them easy to store but have a habit of folding when in use as well. Home made grapnel anchors made of rebar (steel bar used to reinforce construction concrete) are probably the best option in very rocky and snaggy areas as the prongs will bend to allow a snagged anchor to be retrieved, and are cheap to replace if that fails.

**Grapnel Anchor**

All anchors need some additional weight to ensure the pull from the boat is as horizontal as possible, which is what makes them dig in. You need to fix a length of chain, of a thickness proportional to the size of anchor and rope, between the anchor and the main rope. This also prevents the rough seabed chaffing the anchor rope. Rope, chain and anchor need to be joined together with good shackles, greased, screwed tight and secured (or "moused") with cord or preferably stainless wire to prevent them working undone. As a general guide, the length of chain needs to be at least the length of your boat, more if you feel able to haul up the extra weight. Chain is sized according to the diameter of the metal making up the link.

---

**Tip:**

Rig your anchor to self-trip (i.e. release) if it becomes snagged when retrieving. The following method is possible on all types of anchor except Danforth. Firstly, attach the end of the chain to the crown of the anchor instead of the usual fixing point. There will usually be a convenient eye provided on plough and Bruce anchors for this purpose. Find a point on the chain about two links longer that the full length of the stock and eye, and tie the link to the anchor eye with a few turns of light cord. This cord should be strong enough to hold the boat under normal circumstances, but break if the pull exceeds the normal holding strain. If the anchor snags, keep pulling and when the cord breaks, you will be pulling the anchor out backwards and away from the obstruction that snagged it.

---

Anchor rope needs to be of sufficient strength and thickness to hold the boat in rough weather, and of sufficient length so that you can let the anchor rope out a length of at least three times and preferably five times the depth of water you are in. In very deep water, you will not need so much rope because the much higher force of tide on the full length of rope will make the anchor dig in more rather than less.

Don't be tempted to go for thin rope even if it is strong enough, because when hauling by hand a thicker rope is easier to manage. Anchor rope needs to be stretchy to absorb shocks, and non-floating so it helps set the anchor and stay out of the way of propellers at slack tide. Nylon is the best anchor rope, although it is not the cheapest type of rope available. Polyester is an alternative. Three-strand is perfectly adequate, although multi-plait versions are available. The size of a rope is described by the diameter in millimetres.

If you cannot rig your anchor to self-trip and you are fishing an area with a snaggy bottom, it is wise to buoy the anchor. This means attaching a small marker float to the crown of the anchor with a line of sufficient strength to recover the anchor. This line can be much thinner than the main anchor rope as it will not be needed to hold the weight of the boat. If the anchor snags, you can pull the anchor out from the snag backwards with the buoy line.

## Dropping Anchor

If you are anchoring on a general mark, such as a large area of broken ground, then the positioning of your boat at anchor need not be too exact. When you decide to anchor, put the engine in neutral, let the boat come to a halt in the water, unfasten the anchor and pay it out gently – don't throw all the chain and rope out in a heap, or it may tangle on the way down. Make sure the free end is tied to something so that you do not inadvertently pay it all out and lose the lot.

When you feel the anchor touch the bottom, continue to feed rope out as the boat settles back with the wind and tide until a sufficient length of rope has been paid out. With experience, you will know when that is by the angle of the rope as it leaves the boat. You can never put out too much rope, but you can put out too little. If there is not enough rope, the angle of pull on the anchor will cause it break out rather than dig in.

When you think you have enough rope out, make a few turns around your forward bollard or cleat, then finish off with a figure of eight. It is not necessary to tie a knot – in fact it is better not to in case you have to make a fast move such as when you find yourself in the path of a fast-approaching ship! Before you switch off the engine and start fishing, make sure the anchor has started to grip the seabed. If you are near other boats, you can easily tell if you are dragging backwards. To make sure you are not, take hold of the anchor rope. In a running tide, it will be tight as a bar and there will be no other feel other than the "tingling" of the water running past. If the anchor is dragging, you will feel the rope pull and slacken, and you may even feel the rumble of the anchor slipping over the seabed.

There are a number of reasons for dragging. It may be there is not enough rope out, so try letting out more and see if the anchor grips. The anchor chain may have become tangled around the other parts of the anchor, which is a more common occurrence with fisherman anchors. Danforth anchors sometimes get a rock wedged between the flukes preventing it digging in, or a pebble can jam the stock preventing it swivelling correctly and digging in. If the anchor does not set correctly even after letting more rope out, the only solution is to pull it in and start again. Some sea-beds are very difficult to anchor on – in areas of hard, flat rock the only solution is to allow the anchor to drag on a very long rope until the flukes catch on a ledge or crevice.

Once the anchor has set, ensure that the anchor rope is secured over the bows. Never anchor by the stern or side, this is highly dangerous and can result in swamping or capsizing. You can now stop the engine, and start fishing! If you have a GPS and you are concerned about dragging, you can set the Anchor Watch feature. This sounds an alarm if you position changes more than a pre-set distance. Don't set this too short, otherwise it will sound the alarm as the boat swings naturally with the tide – set it to just over twice the length of your anchor rope, then it will not sound even if the tide changes direction. It is highly advisable to set this alarm when night fishing, as it is more difficult to sense anchor drag if you cannot see other objects to keep a visual reference of your position.

If you need to fish over a precise spot such a reef, wreck or bank, your anchoring position needs to be carefully calculated so that the effects of wind and tide do not push you off the intended position. Your tidal atlas will give you an idea of the strength and direction of the tide, and a quick look around will show you which way the wind is blowing. Both of these forces will dictate where the boat settles after the anchor digs in. An experienced skipper can probably estimate where to drop an anchor with a fair degree of accuracy. With the help of a GPS, you can be fairly accurate too.

If you want to fish directly over a reef, firstly locate the reef using GPS and fish-finder. Set the GPS option to "track", and mark the position of the fishing point if the coordinates are not already entered. Put the engine in neutral, and allow the boat to drift. Depending on the type of boat, the effect of wind may be more than the effect of tide. You will be able to see the drift on the GPS screen. Let the boat drift for the length of time it would take to drop and set the anchor, and make a note of the length of drift during that time.

Now put the engine in gear, and motor gently back up the track, and keep going for an equal distance. Continue on for the length of rope you are going to pay out, then make a slight adjustment for the effects of wind if that is necessary – more so for light boats in a cross-wind. The effects of tide will be more significant than the effects of wind once you are anchored, because of the force of the tide on all the anchor rope. Put the engine in neutral, mark the position on the GPS again and anchor as described above. Your anchor will hit the seabed after you have drifted back slightly, and the boat will settle at the end of the rope you have paid out.

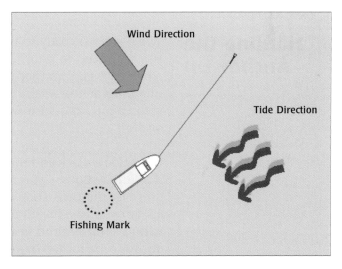

**Anchoring 1**

If you have estimated all the distances and bearings correctly, you will end up just up-tide of your mark. Have a look at the GPS plot screen and see. If you are off-target, then note the relative position of the intended mark with your current position, and try again – this time anchoring in a position offset from your original anchoring position by the same distance and bearing as your original error – this second attempt should put you spot on the mark. This might seem like a lot of trouble, but a mark like a wreck will hold fish in a very localised position – miss it by a few metres and you will miss a lot of fish.

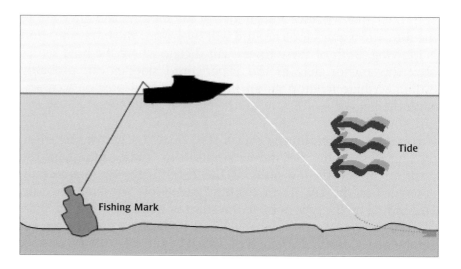

**Anchoring 2**

## Hauling the Anchor Up

When you are ready to move to another mark, or head back home, you will need to haul the anchor in. Firstly, reel in all your lines, remove weights and secure hooks so they do not fly about. Put rods in rod holders or secure them with elastic cords out of the way. Start your engine, and let it warm up on tick-over while you sort out the anchor.

If the tide is slack and the anchor is light this may be simple enough if a little tedious – you can just haul it up. Keep the rope tidy, and don't let the coils stray and tangle – if you suddenly let go of the anchor you don't want to find yourself following it into the depths with a loop around your foot. Some boats have a purpose-built anchor rope locker, or you may coil your rope into a plastic bin. If the anchor locker is fiddly to stow rope in as you haul, fit a large hook such as a life-buoy holder on a rail nearby and loop the rope over the hook as you pull it in. This keeps it tidy until you can tuck it in the locker.

If the tide is running, you will be surprised how difficult it is to pull the anchor up by hand. One way is to have the helmsman motor very slowly up tide as a crew member pulls in the rope. This must be done very carefully to ensure the boat does not run over the rope and tangle the propeller. As the boat goes over the anchor and the rope is vertical to the sea-bed, the anchor will break out of its hold and the boat can be allowed to drift as the rest of the anchor rope is recovered.

Alternatively, if your wallet can stretch to it or the size of the boat justifies it, you can fit an anchor winch. Manual winches may be adequate for yachts anchoring in shallow bays, but they are not really suitable for deep water anchoring. An electric winch is required, and these run to several hundreds of pounds, plus electrics and fitting costs.

Another method uses a large float and a stainless steel ring called an Alderney Ring. There is a branded version on the market called an Anka-Yanka. This method uses the force of the tide and the movement of the boat to lift the anchor, but it should only be used when you have plenty of boat handling experience because it is easy to make a mistake and tangle your propeller. However, when you feel ready for it here is how to do it.

You need a buoy, a large balloon fender or similar of sufficient size to float your entire anchor and chain. These are readily available from yacht chandlers, or cheaper ones can be bought from commercial fishing gear suppliers. You also require a large stainless steel ring of at least 15cm diameter, attached to the buoy with a shackle. To raise the anchor, you pass the anchor line through the ring and let the ring run freely up and down the anchor rope. Some rings are available with a gap and two smaller rings welded either side which makes it is easy to clip the ring to the rope without having to thread the rope through the ring. You could use a loop of rope or a large snap ring but these may not run as freely as a large steel ring.

Throw the buoy into the water, then motor up-tide at an angle of about 30° to the direction of the anchor rope. As you motor forwards, the rope will slacken and make a loop, with the buoy slipping along the rope keeping the apex of the loop on the surface. Keep your eyes on the buoy, and make sure you are not running over the anchor rope. If you lose sight of it, slip into neutral, drop back and try again. You may need to take a wider angle to clear the rope. As you pass the point where the anchor is on the sea-bed, steer slightly back towards the original line of the anchor to follow a shallow arc around the anchor. Keep going, and the anchor will be pulled up to the buoy.

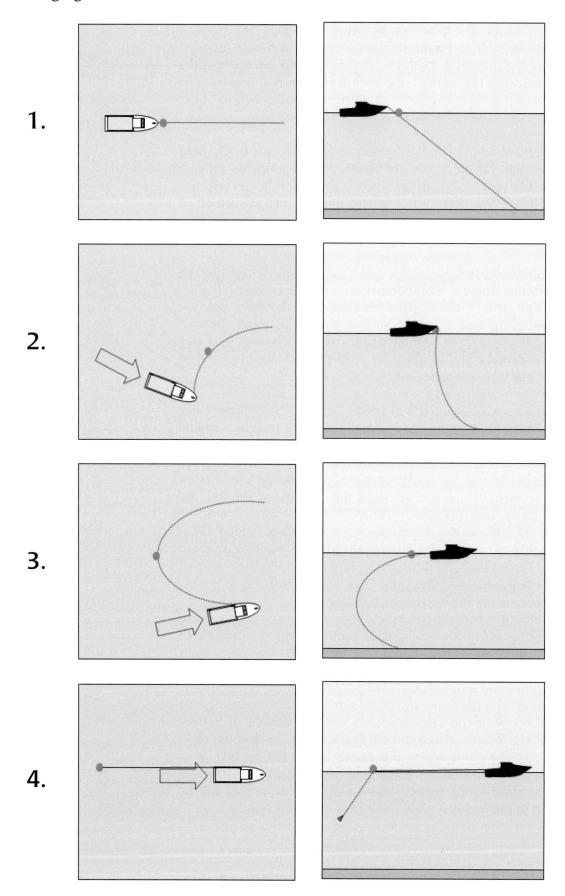

**Alderney Ring**

If the buoy sinks, it was too small! When you think the chain has reached the ring, give a burst of throttle to pull the chain through the ring, and put the engine in neutral. You can now pull the anchor back to the boat very easily, as the weight of anchor and chain is being carried by the buoy.

Once you have recovered the rope, chain, buoy and anchor make everything secure – particularly the anchor, as you don't want that to drop while you are travelling along.

---

Tip:

When you drop anchor, put your buoy and ring on the anchor rope, fix some form of stopper on the rope to prevent the buoy siding up the rope towards the boat (a 30cm length of broom handle clove-hitched to the anchor rope will do), then let out a few more metres of rope. This has three advantages – the buoy is not banging on the boat all day; you are ready to start the engines and immediately up-anchor in case you have to move in a hurry, and also the helmsman will be able to see the buoy at all times making it easier to avoid running over the anchor rope.

---

## Recovering a Snagged Anchor

Sometimes, recovering an anchor does not go according to plan. It may have a fluke caught under a rock, a piece or wreckage or a stray submerged rope. If you have not rigged the anchor to self-trip when pulled hard, or you have put too strong a tie on the self-trip and you cannot break it, your anchor will remain stuck fast. All is not lost however, and there is a way of recovering a plough, Danforth or Bruce anchor if you have some extra rope and chain. This method will not work for a fisherman anchor because of the projecting stock.

Make a loop of a length of chain, a length of about two metres will be sufficient, and take it round the anchor rope and attach both ends of the chain to another length of rope, which is at least twice the depth of water. Pull the anchor rope as tight as possible, the let the chain loop slide down the anchor rope, remembering to tie the free end of the second rope to a strong cleat in the boat. The weight of the chain should take the rope right down the shank of the anchor and settle around the crown. Now tie a buoy to the free end of the anchor line, cast it adrift, and motor up-tide of the anchor. Your chain loop should pull the anchor out from under the snag, which means you can pull it up and recover the anchor, both ropes and the buoy.

If you have a fisherman anchor, or do not have the necessary rope and chain on board, you may be able to free the anchor if the snag is not hard on the sea-bed, such as a ground rope for a string of pots. If you pull the anchor as tight as possible, let it drop back again, then immediately pull it up you might make it fall free of the snag. Alternatively, you could ask for help from a larger vessel who may be able to pull the anchor out from the snag by brute force, although the anchor may end up bent or the rope break.

If all these attempts fail, your only choice is to recover the buoy and abandon the anchor, or to leave the anchor buoyed and persuade members of a friendly diving club to recover it for you.

# VHF Radios

Your VHF radio is one of the most important items in your boat, both for safety and to communicate with other anglers while you are at sea. If you own a boat with a VHF set you must pass an operator's examination and hold a VHF operator's certificate before you can use it. This section is not a substitute for a course, but it will give you some basic guidelines in preparation for owning and operating a VHF set.

VHF stands for "Very High Frequency", and for UK marine use covers the frequencies between 156MHz and 162MHz. Sets are available for permanent fixing in a boat, and portable handheld units are available which perform similar functions and have the advantage that they can be carried from boat to boat.

## Types of VHF Radio

Fixed sets require a power supply from the boat battery, and also need a separate, external aerial. This means the power can be greater, and sets can usually be switched between low power (1 Watt) and high power (25 Watts) depending on the distance over which you want to transmit your message. Messages transmitted by VHF travel in straight lines, so the range is limited not only by the power of the transmitter, but also the height of the transmitting and receiving aerials relative to the curvature of the earth. The range of a VHF set is approximately one mile per output watt, assuming a direct line of sight. To maximise the range, it is best to have your VHF aerial mounted as high as possible on the boat. Aerials for power boats are usually at least 2 metres long, made of fibreglass and mounted on a hinged bracket. Longer ones are available, and you can gain extra height by mounting them on a mast or radar arch on the wheelhouse roof.

Unlike a telephone, the VHF radio channels are open to anyone to listen to, so your conversations are not private. A new technology called Digital Selective Calling (DSC) has been introduced and in due course all sets must support DSC. If your set has DSC, you can obtain a MMSI number which is unique to your set. Having MMSI numbers means you can alert the vessel you are calling by transmitting their specific number, much like dialling a phone number. Once they have received the alert, the conversation will still be on the open channels.

A significant advantage of the DSC sets is that you can link them to your GPS set with a cable so the VHF set always has a record of your current position. There are a series of standards defined by the National Marine Electronics Association to exchange data between pieces of navigational equipment, and the instructions in the relevant manuals will refer to a NMEA cable. It is a very simple job to connect a GPS and VHF set – there are only two or three wires that have to be connected and the manuals will show which ones.

A DSC VHF radio will have an emergency button, usually protected by a cover, which when activated will automatically send a distress signal with your MMSI number and your exact position. The Coastguard will know which vessel has that number, so they will know that you are in trouble, where you are and which boat you are in without any further communication. They will also transmit an acknowledgement to the call so you will know they have heard your distress message. This is a huge advantage over the old method of relying on a person to listen for faint distress messages on Channel 16!

Hand-held VHF radios have their own short aerials attached, and have inbuilt rechargeable batteries. This means their power and range is much more limited, and the transmission power is usually only 5 Watts. They are useful for inshore work and as a back-up for the fixed set in case you lose power or the main aerial, but they should not be relied on as your only VHF set if you are going several miles offshore.

## Licensing

If you use a VHF set, you must either hold a current operator's licence or be supervised by someone who has one. This is because there are strict rules and protocol for using the VHF channels to prevent confusion or obstruction of other users. VHF channels are used by the Coastguard, search and rescue teams, port operations and ship to ship communication by the professionals as well as anglers and yachtsmen. Courses are run by the RYA, independent organisations and evening classes are even available in many adult education centres around the country. The final examination is part theory, part practical where you demonstrate that you know what you are doing with a VHF set and can use it effectively in both normal use and emergency situations.

A licence is also required for the boat itself. It is renewed annually, and all you have to do is ensure your set is installed and operating correctly, and you maintain the correct ownership and use information on the central database. You can request and be allocated a MMSI number if you have a fixed DSC set, and all vessels will be allocated a Call Sign. This Call Sign is a series of letters and numbers unique to the vessel, for example **"MJXP6"** which stays with the vessel for its entire life. You can use either the Call Sign or the name of your vessel to identify yourself when transmitting a message.

The marine VHF frequencies are divided up into channels, and each channel is numbered and allocated to a specific purpose. Your VHF set will be pre-tuned to these channels so you can select them with one of the controls on your set. You can download the current channel allocation from a number of sites on the Web. VHF channels are mostly "Simplex", which means only one transmission can be heard at a time. If you are transmitting, you will not be able to hear any other vessel transmitting. This means you have to "take turns" to speak, which is why you say "Over" at the end of your transmission, letting the other party know that you have finished and it is their turn to speak. The transmission power is also significant – a high power transmission will drown a nearby low power transmission, so if you are transmitting to a nearby vessel, use the low power setting. This combination of power and simplex can cause a problem on a channel. If there is a fault on a set or the transmit button is jammed in the on position, the set can transmit "carrier" which will prevent any other person from using that channel. It is also difficult for the Coastguard to alert the vessel causing the problem because of the simplex channel, so it is important that all users of VHF make sure the channel is clear after they have used it.

One channel is reserved exclusively as a calling channel and for distress calls – Channel 16. There is usually a button on the radio that allows you to hop directly to that channel. There may be another button that allows you to listen to both Channel 16 and other channels by scanning rapidly between them. All vessels with a VHF radio are obliged to monitor Channel 16. To call another vessel, you first call them on Channel 16, then when they acknowledge, the person called nominates a working channel and you both switch to that channel to continue the conversation.

Channel 67 is reserved as a working channel for the Coastguard. You first call them on Channel 16, then they will ask you to transfer to Channel 67. Other channels are used for safety information, port operations and ship to ship. There are also channels allocated for marina use – your chart, marina information and sometimes a sign on a post will tell you on which channel to call a marina as you arrive.

In the event of a Mayday call or similar emergency, all other users must stay clear of Channel 16 until the Coastguard have completed the Mayday co-ordination or transferred to another channel such as Channel 67. The Coastguard will broadcast the instruction "Seelance Mayday" which effectively means keep off Channel 16 unless you are part of rescue co-ordination.

If you have a DSC set it may sound an alarm tone, which either means someone who knows your MMSI number is calling you, or the Coastguard has a safety information broadcast. Sometimes this

# VHF Channels

is a routine weather update; sometimes it can be a special message such as warning of a missing buoy, drifting wreckage or a large vessel manoeuvring.

More information on VHF channels and how to use them will be provided on your VHF course. Don't be tempted to skip the course, it is well worth the little time it takes and knowledge of VHF procedures could save your life or that of others.

| Type | Characteristics | Uses |
|---|---|---|
| **3-strand Nylon** | Sinks. A high stretch characteristic makes this line exceptionally good at absorbing shock loads. Easy to splice with soft eyes or thimbles. Excellent abrasion resistance. Very good UV resistance. Not very acid-proof. Tends to go stiff when wet, particularly in the larger 3-strand sizes. | Ideal for anchor warps and mooring lines |
| **3-strand Polyester** | Sinks. Even when wet it retains full strength and remains easy to handle. Good abrasion resistance. Easy to splice with soft eyes or thimbles. Flexible and soft to handle. Nearly as strong as nylon, but not so much stretch. It can be braided or pre-stretched to give very low stretch. Excellent UV resistance. Very good chemical resistance. | Can be used for anchor warps, mooring warps, lanyards, fenders and fender lines |
| **Double-braided Dockline** | Designed specifically for mooring lines, more strength than 3 strand mooring lines. Shock absorbing braided nylon core, abrasion resistant polyester cover. Stronger than 3-strand ropes, easy to handle and splice. | Specially designed for mooring lines |

# Ropes and Knots

Ropes and knots almost symbolise boating – the special names for marine ropes and knots are often used to caricature life at sea. It need not be so mysterious however, as you only really need to know a few knots and the main types of man-made rope available.

The ropes that are used for normal applications on small power boats are listed below. You will find marine ropes are almost exclusively man-made; natural fibres such as sisal and hemp are used only on traditional craft and for decoration. Ropes for sailing boat applications are not included here – you will discover a great variety in your yacht chandlers. Have a look in the off-cut bins, you can usually find reasonably-priced hanks of a useful length for small boats.

All ropes will unravel if cut. To prevent this, they are cut at the chandlers with a hot knife. If you want to trim a man-made fibre rope yourself, wrap tape around to prevent it unravelling, cut the rope with a sharp knife and melt the end with a flame or soldering iron. Wet your fingers and mould the end into a neat shape while it is still pliant.

## Rope

| Type | Characteristics | Uses |
| --- | --- | --- |
| **Multiplait Nylon** | Sinks. Very flexible making it easy to stow in the chain locker without kinking. Provides elasticity with flexibility. Absorbs high shock loads and is easily spliced. | Specially designed for anchor warps, mooring warps and mooring risers. |
| **Polypropylene** | Floats. Not so strong as nylon or polyester. Stretch is between nylon and polyester, depending on type. Excellent chemical resistance. Not very resistance to UV. Satisfactory wear resistance, depending on type. | Because it is stiff, not particularly easy to tie and floats, it is best to use this type only for a floating rescue line. |
| **Polyethylene** | Floats. Similar properties to monofilament polypropylene. | Used mainly in the fishing industry. Useful for cheap pot-lines but requires leaded inserts to ensure it sinks |

## Ropes

## Knots

A good knowledge of a few key knots is essential if you use a boat. If you do not tie a knot correctly, the rope could easily come undone, or jam, at an awkward moment. Depending on circumstances this could be embarrassing or downright dangerous.

You only need to know a few knots, and these are easy to tie. If you use the correct knots you will not only make boating safer and easier for yourself, you will show other, more knowledgeable boaters that you are one of the boating fraternity and not just an angler on a boat!

### Clove Hitch

The clove hitch is used to tie a rope to a post or rail. It is a useful knot for this purpose as the rope under load can be let in and out under control by untying only the first part of the hitch. It is used for tying fender ropes to rails, and mooring lines to posts.

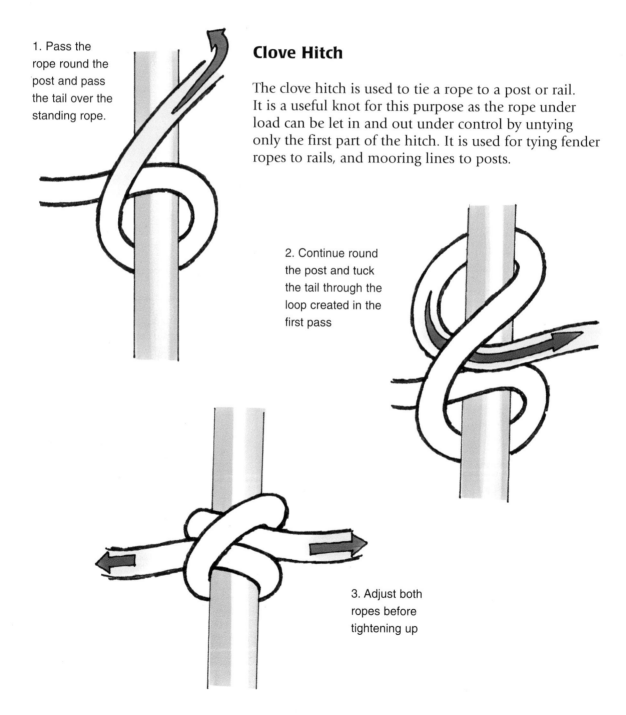

1. Pass the rope round the post and pass the tail over the standing rope.

2. Continue round the post and tuck the tail through the loop created in the first pass

3. Adjust both ropes before tightening up

# Round Turn and Two Half Hitches

The round turn and two half hitches is a good knot for tying a rope to a ring or post when it is expected to take a heavy strain. The round turn helps secure the rope and takes some of the strain before the hitches take it, which means the hitches do not tighten as much as they would without the round turns, and are consequently easier to untie after the load is released.

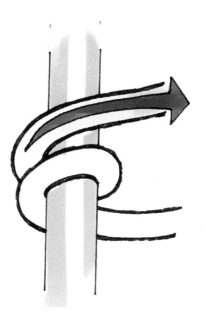

1. Make two turns around a ring or post.

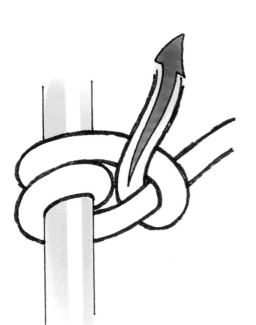

2. Tie one half hitch by passing the tail around the standing rope and through the loop.

3. Make a second half hitch by repeating this, then pull tight.

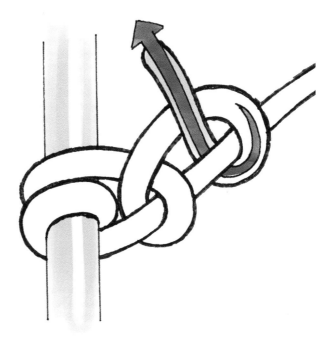

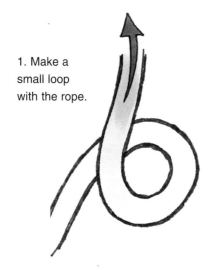

1. Make a
small loop
with the rope.

## Bowline

A bowline loop cannot slip, so it is a good loop to use if you need to keep a loop of a fixed size, such as on the end of a mooring line or a safely line around a person. It does become very tight after a load is applied to it, but it can be undone by twisting the knot.

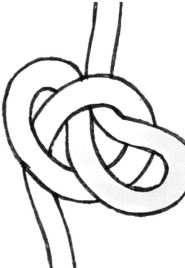

2. Twist this loop around and pull a small section of the standing part of the rope through the loop.

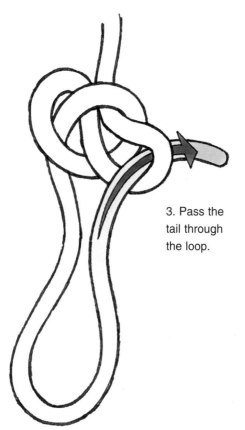

3. Pass the tail through the loop.

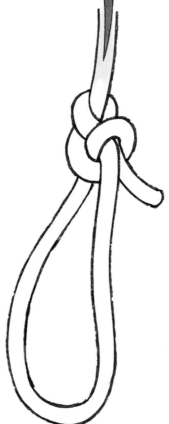

4. Pull the standing part of the rope to pull the tail through the loop, leaving the free end outside the loop. Tighten and snug the knot down.

## Cleat Hitch

A cleat is a very useful fixing point, but you need to know how to tie a rope to it. It is very good for taking considerable strain from the rope and remaining very easy to untie.

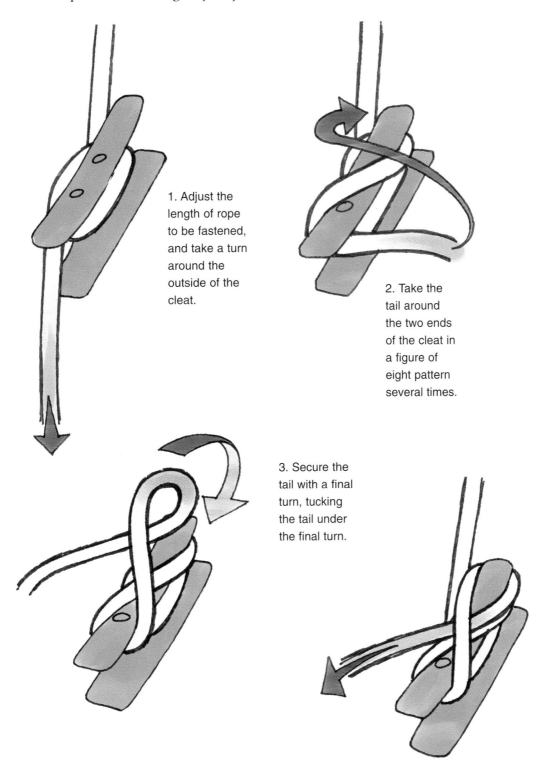

1. Adjust the length of rope to be fastened, and take a turn around the outside of the cleat.

2. Take the tail around the two ends of the cleat in a figure of eight pattern several times.

3. Secure the tail with a final turn, tucking the tail under the final turn.

## Double Sheet Bend

A sheet bend is used to tie two ropes together, and works just as well for two ropes of differing types or thickness. It looks very simple but it is much more secure than a reef or granny knot, neither of which are of much use on a power boat.

1. Make a loop at the end of the first rope - the thicker if they are not of the same thickness.

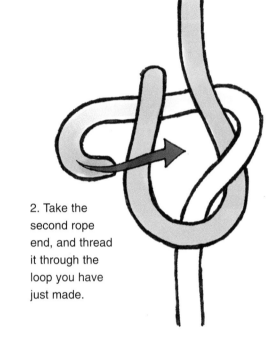

2. Take the second rope end, and thread it through the loop you have just made.

3. Pass the second rope around the back of the loop and round to the front, and tuck the tail under the second rope and over the loop of the first rope.

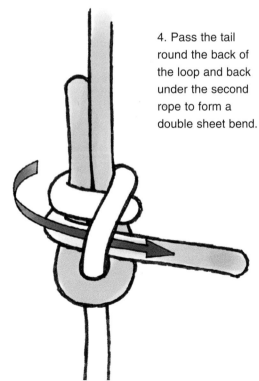

4. Pass the tail round the back of the loop and back under the second rope to form a double sheet bend.

# Looking After Yourself

The safety and comfort of you and your crew are just as important as the boat itself – it is no use having the perfect boat but finding you are cold and miserable. A few precautions can help you enjoy your trips to the full.

## Clothing

This might seem obvious, but make sure you are dressed appropriately for the season. The temperature at sea can be surprisingly cold even in summer, so make sure you take plenty of additional layers to add – or take off. In winter, thermal underwear and thermal socks are the norm: there is no point being a fashion victim and suffering from the cold. A t-shirt, thick shirt, sweatshirt, fleece and snug gives you plenty of combinations to cover the full range of UK temperatures!

Waterproof over-jacket and trousers are essential. Even in dry weather, over-trousers keep your legs dry from splashes, and free from fish or bait slime. Heavy duty yachting clothing is a better investment than camping and hiking gear – it is designed for the environment you will be fishing in, and will be warm, waterproof and hard-wearing. I like bib-and-brace style trousers, these keep you warmer and dryer than waist trousers.

In the colder seasons from autumn to spring, I recommend a flotation suit. These are available as one-piece or two piece suits, and include insulation and buoyancy to help you maintain body temperature and stay afloat in cold water. If you wear one while fishing you can chose not to wear a life-jacket, although the suit may not keep an unconscious person in the same position as a life-jacket would. The insulating properties make winter fishing much more comfortable, and would be a life-saver if you were unfortunate enough to end up in the water as they will inhibit the effects of hypothermia for many minutes.

Footwear is also important. Your feet must have a secure grip on a wet, sloping deck and yachting shoes or boots are the best. Whatever the temptation on a sunny day, I would advise against going barefoot or even wearing sandals – there are many hard objects on a boat to stub toes or worse, and there have been several reported occurrences of toes being bitten off by conger while on deck.

A hat is also advisable – a cap in summer to protect the scalp from sun; a waterproof hat or hood for rainy weather and a fleece beanie for colder days. Gloves for very cold days will make fishing bearable; either neoprene gloves with flip-off fingers or mittens which can be removed easily are the best – you will need to switch from having fingers free for knotting or baiting, to keeping hands warm while waiting for a bite.

## Sun Protection

In recent years there has been a significantly increased awareness of the dangers of exposing our skin to the harmful effects of the sun. On open water, those effects are increased because of the length of exposure in an un-shaded boat cockpit, and the reflection of the sun's rays from the water adds to the effects of the sun directly. It is easy to underestimate the strength of the sun because the air temperature at sea in a gentle breeze will be comfortably low even in peak summer months.

Your skin can be damaged in any month of the year, and a sunny day as early as April and as late as October can result in sunburn if precautions are not taken. Sunburn can not only be painful, the damage to skin cannot be repaired and is a common cause of skin cancer.

A good sun protection lotion should be on your boat at all times, not just for yourself but also for guests who may not realise how severe the sun can be. All exposed skin should be liberally smothered with a high factor, waterproof sun cream of at least Factor 30 and preferably more. In the sunniest months, total sun block on the nose, cheekbones and forehead is standard practice with race yacht crews and there is every reason to follow their example. There are some good sport-branded sun lotions designed for men so there is no reason any more to think sun protection is for pansies.

Sunglasses are a must in all seasons. In summer, glare from the water can be very strong and you must protect your eyes with good quality glasses. In winter, the sun can be very low in the sky and you may have to steer into the glare. Finding your way home up a narrow channel heading west on a dry winter evening can be nearly impossible without good sunglasses.

## Sea Sickness

Some people are lucky and are never affected, some are never able to set foot in a boat without feeling queasy, but most people are susceptible from time to time. There is no guaranteed quick cure, but there are plenty of medications ranging from prescription to quirky.

There are Dramamine patches which are available either on prescription or over the counter in some countries. There are a number of brands of travel sickness tablets available, Stugeron and Kwells being very popular. You may have to try different ones to find one that works for you. Whatever the medication, follow the instructions carefully and if it says take them before travelling, do so because they are preventative drugs, not cures. If you feel sick, it is too late.

Sea-Bands and similar devices use pressure points on the wrist or electrical pulses to suppress sea-sickness. They seem strange but plenty swear by them, and they do not have side-effects. Long term they are much cheaper than drugs although they might seem expensive initially.

You can also take precautions in advance to prevent seasickness. If you go to sea with a hangover, or have a few too many the night before, you are far more likely to feel sick. Tiredness, stress and unfamiliar diet can also bring it on. Make sure you feel fresh and at your best physically before you go and you stand the best choice of enjoying the day. Your body will get used to the motion of the sea – a few trips in a gentle sea before going out in a Force 5 will give you a better chance of seeing the rougher trip through.

If you think you may be queasy, avoid the cabin and stay out in the fresh air where you can keep an eye on the horizon. Make up traces before you go, so you do not have to spend time peering down at knots – if you get in a tangle, cut the line and tie on a new rig rather than risk feeling sick. Keep drinking water, and eating non-greasy food like biscuits and bread will help keep your stomach in order.

Other tricks I have heard of, but cannot vouch for, are eating ginger biscuits, drinking cider and sticking plaster behind the ears! Stugeron, Sea-Bands and avoiding tiredness work best for me, but everyone is different. The best tip is to go fishing a lot and get used to the motion – a good tip for two reasons!

# Food and Drink

If you plan to be out even for a short time, be sure to take plenty to drink, particularly in hot weather. In cold weather take a thermos of a hot drink as well, if you do not have cooking facilities on board. The more expensive stainless steel unbreakable flasks are worth the money – traditional vacuum flasks have a short life in a boat at sea. Despite the temptations, it is best to avoid alcohol at sea. You will need sound judgement at all times, and many of the people who drown from falling from boats had been drinking beforehand. It is not worth the risk.

If you have a boat with a cabin or enclosed wheelhouse, you may want to install cooking facilities even if you just want to boil a kettle. There are two types of stove suitable for a small boat – gas powered or liquid fuelled. Both are dangerous to have in a boat if the correct precautions are not taken. If you are buying a stove, make sure it is designed for use in a boat – it will have features to prevent spillage, and will be made of rust-resistant materials. Cheap camping stoves are not suitable.

Tip:

Have a look round your supermarket for food items that can be kept without the need for a fridge, and can make a filling meal with simple heating. Cuppa-soups are good; instant cappuccino coffee saves taking milk; tins of beans and sausages, stews, "big" soups, chilli and tinned pasta in sauces are all useful. If your cooking can extend to a five minute simmer, there are packs of dried pasta complete with sauce available. The ubiquitous Pot Noodles are every angler's standby. Processed foods have a high salt content so make sure you have plenty to drink with you.

Stoves must be fitted so they cannot fall from their position, and have rails called "fiddles" to prevent kettles and saucepans sliding off as the boat heels. If the heat generated by the stove is likely to damage the area above and near it, the area must be protected with insulated, flame-proof sheeting which is available from the more specialised yacht chandlers.

Classic pressurised paraffin stoves are favoured by traditionalists, but these are fiddly to operate and personally I don't feel comfortable near pressurised fuel and a naked flame. A better choice is the un-pressurised liquid fuel stove such as those manufactured by Origo. These have a non-spill fuel reservoir underneath; you simply fill the reservoir with methylated spirits or de-natured alcohol, and light it. These stoves are surprisingly effective for such a simple design, and are one of the safest types. The only real danger is in re-filling. Make sure the flame is out and there are no sparks or hot-spots before you open the stove to re-fill. If the bottle of meths caught fire in your hands you would be very badly injured.

An alternative fuel is gas. The problem with gas in a boat is that it is heavier than air, therefore leaked gas will sink to the bottom of the boat rather than drifting away, and lie there as an invisible explosive cloud waiting for a spark to ignite it. This risk can be minimised by making a fully enclosed gas cabinet with a drain-hole over the side so leaked gas will drain into the atmosphere instead of the bilges. Make sure gas cocks are switched off when the stove is not in use to prevent leakage from pipes and burners. If you take these precautions, gas stoves are safe enough and you can enjoy hot food on your trips.

# If Things Go Wrong

If you take all the sensible precautions, you can have many pleasant days fishing from your boat in safety. But however careful you are, sometimes something may go wrong. At sea, you are a long way from assistance even if you are only a few hundred yards from shore – unlike on land, you cannot start walking for help. You need to be prepared for emergencies that may occur despite your best preparations. This means not only having the correct equipment on board, but also knowing what to do, and what not to do. Even if nothing untoward ever happens to you, you will be in a very good position to help someone else in difficulties.

Medical emergencies can be the result of illness, such as a heart attack, or injury caused by falling, a knife cut or even a bite from an angry conger eel. There is no substitute for a course in First Aid, this can give you the confidence to deal with most situations until more expert help arrives.

## Medical Emergencies

A first aid pack should always be carried, and the contents need to be geared to the likely needs at sea. Plasters, wound flushing sachets and antiseptic will help with the less critical cuts and abrasions. You should also pack bandages and wound pads in case of more serous injury. Bandages can also be used to make makeshift splints in case you have to stabilise someone with a broken bone in a moving boat. Serious bleeding, broken bones, concussion and hypothermia are far more serious and help must be requested through the Coastguard. If the problem is life threatening, do not hesitate to send out a Mayday. The Coastguard will tell you what to do and send assistance. If it is serious but not life threatening, use "Pan Pan Medico" as your emergency alert and the coastguard will connect you with a hospital doctor who will talk you through what you need to do, and help will be sent if it is needed quicker than you can make the journey back to an accessible landing place.

> Tip:
>
> Weevers are the only fish commonly caught in UK waters that have stinging spines. They frequent shallow, sandy bottoms and are often caught by anglers targeting flatfish. A sting is very painful, but not life threatening unless there are other complications. One way to prevent the poison spreading and causing increased pain is to apply the hottest water the patient can stand on the place of the sting. This causes the poison to gel and prevents it from spreading within the body. Beach Life Guards carry thermos flasks of hot water for this purpose.

There are many good first aid booklets available, and even if you have taken a course on first aid one will be useful to have on board in case you are the one in trouble, or in case you need to remind yourself of the correct action to take in the turmoil of a sudden medical emergency.

## Man Overboard

Falling overboard is one of the most common causes of death for leisure boaters – and is far more common than going into the water as a result of sinking or capsize. Sudden immersion has serious consequences for the human body even in summer, because the water temperature is much lower than air temperature and body temperature. Most people are aware of the dangers of hyperthermia, which is the result of prolonged lowering of the body temperature resulting in drowsiness and loss of consciousness. Fewer people are aware of the danger of Cold Water Shock, which is a much quicker killer.

When someone falls into cold water – and the water temperature around the UK in June can be only 10°C – they will experience rapid, shallow breathing with increased heartbeat and blood pressure. This involuntary reaction is very dangerous because it can cause the person to inhale water and drown, even though they may be very fit and excellent swimmers. Fortunately this effect only lasts a few minutes, so make sure if you fall in you stay still and calm for two or three minutes before trying to swim.

The boat-handling and recovery aspect of a man-overboard incident has been covered in earlier sections. Once you have the casualty back on board, make sure they are kept warm. This is where a survival bag can be vital. When the body temperature drops to 35°C the casualty develops hypothermia, and below 30°C it can be fatal. If practical, remove wet clothing and cover the casualty with blankets and a survival bag. If the casualty is unconscious, loosen clothing around the neck and chest and place him in the recovery position with the head lower than the body. If you have any concerns about the medical condition of the casualty, call the Coastguard, and most definitely do so if they are unconscious.

Secondary drowning can occur after the casualty is recovered, and even up to several hours afterwards. This is caused by the lungs or throat swelling up or going into spasm as a result of irritation and thus preventing air from reaching the lungs. Even if the casualty appears to be recovering well, keep a close eye on them and if they complain of shortness of breath, coughing or chest pain get medical help immediately.

## Breakdown

There can be many reasons for losing motive power – engine failure, fuel, gearbox, propeller or coolant problems. As the sea is a cold and lonely place, and wind and tide may be taking you into danger, you need to know what to do to minimise the dangers and make sure you get under way again or get home safely.

If you have a sudden loss of power or the engine stops, it is tempting to immediately look for the problem. There is something else you must do first – take stock of where you are and how much sea room you have. Assess the tide, wind, depth of water and other boat traffic and decide whether you can afford to drift for a few minutes or you need to anchor. If you are in a main shipping lane on no account must you anchor – unless you think you can resolve the problem very quickly you must call the Coastguard on Channel 16 and when asked to, switch to Channel 67 and explain the situation to them. They can then decide whether to send help, divert a port operations vessel or warn other shipping using the channel.

If you think you have room to drift for a while, keep a good lookout all the time, or better still, allocate one of your crew to lookout duties. You can drift upon a string of lobster pots very suddenly and you would not want a tangle with a pot rope to add to your problems.

If you are likely to drift onto rocks or banks, or into a shipping channel, and if the water is shallow enough it is better to drop anchor while you try and fix the problem or wait for help. Make sure the water you are in is not too shallow – if the tide drops and you are in very shallow water, other boats will not be able to get near to tow you. Do not be tempted to head for a beach thinking it is a place of safety – it is not. Even gentle waves will pound your boat on the sand or shingle, and if there are rocks, groyns or other objects the hull can be quickly holed. Even if you were able to beach without damage or broaching in the surf, you will probably not be in a very good position to receive further help. The boat could not be recovered unless there was a slipway leading to the beach, and it would not be easy for another boat to tow your boat off the beach. Unless you are in such a bad situation that you need to save lives and are prepared to allow your boat to become an insurance "total loss", avoid beaches!

Tip:

There are a growing number of marine breakdown services operating around areas of high marine leisure activity, particularly along the South Coast of England. These operate in a similar way to the AA or RAC, where for an annual subscription you can call on the services of an engineer in a fast RIB to come to your aid. Depending on distance and other calls you may have to wait some time so make sure you can anchor. Many also offer the services of a diver to untangle ropes from propellers, although for safety reasons this would only be possible in sheltered water.

An engine breakdown is not a justification for a Mayday unless your boat and crew is in imminent and serious danger, such as a breakdown where you could quickly be swept onto dangerous rocks. By all means alert the Coastguard, they will be happy to monitor the situation and alert other nearby boats that could provide help or a tow.

A common cause of breakdown, particularly near major ports and densely populated areas, is the good old plastic bag. These float just below the surface, and bin liners and fertiliser sacks are big enough to envelope the propeller of even the larger fishing boats you are likely to be operating. The first symptom of a large bag pick-up is often a sudden reduction in power – although the engine revolutions may still be high, the propeller can no longer push the water as it was designed to do. This in itself is irritating, but there may be a more serious underlying problem.

On outboard and out-drive legs, the cooling water pick-up point is on the leg just in front of the propeller – just where a bag may wrap itself. This can block the intake ports and starve the engine of cooling water. Water pumps are not designed to run dry, and even a few seconds of running with no water in the cooling system can wreck the pump. If you suspect a bag is the culprit, stop the engine immediately and lift the leg to clear the obstruction. Never lift an out-drive leg with the engine running – this will damage the drive system.

Modern marine engines are very complex, but also very sophisticated. This means they are less likely to go wrong, but when they do, it often requires more knowledge or parts than the average amateur mechanic is likely to have to hand. There are some basic items that can get you out of trouble however – spanners, screwdrivers and pliers to tighten fastenings that have become loose; tape and wire to hold things together and repair split pipes; WD-40 to spray on dampened electrics; fine emery paper to clean electrical contacts and a set of fuses to replace blown ones.

There are some good day or evening courses available, usually in or near coastal towns, that will teach you basic "get you home" mechanical and electrical repairs for most types of marine engine. A little bit of knowledge is invaluable, but will never teach you all you need to know – experience teaches you more. Here are a few of my own experiences that show that you cannot anticipate everything:

- The engine on a petrol out-drive suddenly cut after I ran through the wake of a passing boat. The sudden jolt had knocked off the plastic plug holding all the wiring to the back of the ignition switch. That took some finding.

- One morning, all the instruments were reading back to front – high was low and low was high. This even defeated the electrician from the boatyard. It turned out to be the main wiring loom plug above the engine – a couple of poor contacts caused strange things to happen.

- Returning from a trip one day the engine suddenly raced, as if the propeller had fallen off – but it was still there. At low speeds the engine worked perfectly, at higher revs the engine would race again. The propeller had a shock-absorbing rubber sleeve bonded between the hub and the blades. The bonding had come loose, which meant there was only enough grip to drive the propeller at low speeds. I was able to make the six miles home – at two knots!

- On a friend's boat, a passing boat sent a wash towards the stern and the outboard cut. We tried everything to get it started to no avail, and were fortunate enough to receive a tow all the way back to the slipway. Next morning the engine started first time, and has run perfectly ever since, even in similar circumstances.

## Auxiliary Engines

The decision to fit a second means of propulsion is a sensible one, but it is easy to fit a small outboard engine and assume you are covered. It is worth thinking carefully about what to take – or even whether to take one at all. The purpose of an auxiliary engine is to get you to safety – even if that is not all the way home – if your main engine fails. If it can't do that, there is little point having one.

If you have an outboard, a smaller outboard can be carried on the transom and used in an emergency. Make sure the small outboard has enough power to move the boat at a useful speed – if it will only move the boat at three knots it is unlikely to get you home from a distant mark, especially if the weather is against you. Also make sure you have an adequate fuel supply for the auxiliary. The reason for the main engine failure could be fuel problems, so the back-up engine should have its own fuel.

If you have an inboard or out-drive, the auxiliary will have to be mounted on a bracket. If it is not kept on the bracket, make sure it is possible to fit it on the bracket at sea in a good wave – if you can't easily do that, you may as well leave it at home.

Having had experience of underpowered auxiliary engines, my own preference is to fit twin outboards rather than one large one and one small. This is a more expensive option but it is the safest: I replaced a 50HP outboard with two 30HP units. I also had two fuel supplies and two batteries giving complete peace of mind.

Moving to diesel power made me completely re-think the question of an auxiliary engine. Modern marine diesels are so much more reliable than petrol engines, I rarely travel more than ten miles from land, I usually fish in the company of other boats, I have two VHF sets and I subscribe to Sea-Start. A secondary engine capable of pushing a 23 foot planing hull would be impractical, so I don't have one. Just to give additional confidence, I went on a diesel engine trouble-shooting course. Plenty of commercial boats rely on a single diesel engine. However, the choice is yours, but make sure you weigh up the options and risks before you decide to invest in a second engine or not.

## Towing

You may need to be towed, or you may be in a position to offer another boat a tow, so some knowledge in this area will be useful. There are two ways of towing depending on the weather and the amount of manoeuvrability required: the traditional "pull", or tying up alongside and travelling as one unit.

The traditional tow suits any weather conditions and is the easiest, but does not offer much if any control if the towed boat has to be taken back to a jetty in a crowded harbour. To prepare for a tow, make sure both parties know what is planned by discussing it on the radio. The anchor rope makes a good tow rope as it is strong and long – mooring warps are not usually long enough.

The towing points on both boats must be substantial – they will be put through significant stress so they must be securely fastened to a strong point in the boat. If you are worried about this, make a "cradle" by fastening a rope linking up several mooring points on the boat to spread the load or act as a backup in case the first point breaks. You can even put the rope right around the wheelhouse or cuddy, but be careful not to prevent doors from opening.

Once the tow has been passed, keep the line taut and in sight to prevent loose line sinking and fouling a propeller. The best approach is for the end of the rope to be secured to the towed boat first, then put a single turn of the rope around a cleat in the towing boat. As the boat moves ahead, let some line out and when there is a safe gap between the two boats, gradually increase the tension so they tow does not "snatch". Let some more line slip out, take a second turn round the cleat then as the towed boat starts to follow you can secure the end. In very bad weather, if the rope is being jerked badly to the point where it may break or pull the tow points out, you can tie a heavy weight such as an anchor to the centre of the tow line to act as a shock absorber. This is easier said than done in heavy weather.

Keep an eye on the towed boat and ensure the speed is not causing it to yaw from side to side – boats are designed to be pushed by a propeller and do not usually take kindly to being pulled from the front.

In very calm waters, and particularly if you want to take the towed boat alongside a jetty or pontoon, the two boats need to be tied together side by side. First put out plenty of fenders to prevent damage, then fasten two ropes to attach bow to bow and stern to stern, and another, substantial rope from the bow of the towing boat to the stern of the towed boat. This is the rope that will take most of the strain of the tow. Roped together like this, both boats can be manoeuvred as one, albeit rather clumsily, but at least you will be able to bring both alongside a pontoon even in a crowded harbour or marina.

---

Tip:

The law of Salvage still applies today. If you accept help from another boat, and particularly if that help prevents the total loss of your boat, the rescuing boat can claim Salvage Rights equivalent to a significant proportion of the value of your boat. If possible when accepting help, agree terms before the rescue work starts. It is difficult to negotiate afterwards.

---

# Swamping or Flooding

The boat's hull is designed to keep water out, but sometimes water gets in: either over the top from a large breaking wave, through integrity failure in the hull – which means something that is supposed to be watertight turns out not to be watertight – or through hull damage.

To avoid sinking, you must firstly prevent more water coming in, then get the water that is in the boat out of it. Correct action taken quickly can prevent the situation becoming worse and potentially disastrous.

If you have taken water over the side as a result of a passing boat wash, or you ended up broadside or stern to a steep wave, you will need to prevent more water coming aboard by turning the boat towards the waves. If your crew are able, they need to start bailing immediately because the additional weight of water will lower the freeboard and make further water ingress more likely. Having stabilised the boat against the waves, you can concentrate on bailing.

All boats should have electric bilge pumps, and a manual pump as a backup is recommended. A huge wave dumping a foot of water in the cockpit will take any pump a while to deal with, and the fastest way to get the water out is with a trusty bucket. Two or three men bailing with buckets can remove a lot of water very quickly.

Once the water is under control you need to assess the damage. If you are lucky the worst may be a fright and a soaking. You may also have suffered water damage to battery and electrics – a spray with WD-40 may resolve the problem, but if not you may need to summon help if you are left without engine power.

Water ingress through hull damage or a component failure is more dangerous because it will be more difficult to prevent more water coming in – it may end up as a race between water coming in and the speed at which you can bail it out. Common integrity problems are caused by structural failure – gaps opening up between hull and outboard well; through-hull mountings such as sea-cocks and speedo impellor failing; and rubber gaiters on out-drive legs splitting. Some outboard powered boats have an access hatch in the outboard well. I have known of more than one near-sinking caused by these giving way and this results in a huge hole opening up – even though this is usually above water level, the slop of waves into the well drives a large quantity of water into the hole and as the boat becomes heavier and settles, more comes in.

If at all possible, try and stop or slow down the leak by jamming anything suitable over the hole. If the hole is on the inside and well below the water line, the water will be under pressure and trying to push your repairs away. If the problem is a missing hatch, try and cover the hole from above so the water pressure helps seal the gap. Use whatever you can, you can always repair and replace when you get home – but your first objective is to get home.

If you think there is a possibility you cannot contain the leak, call the Coastguard immediately and tell them what is going on. If you lose your electrics and VHF later on at least they will know where you are and what is happening. They would prefer to have help standing by or on its way to you, and that could save valuable time if the situation became worse.

A common way of rescuing a small boat that is sinking is to tie it securely alongside a much larger boat. A fishing boat may be diverted to your assistance, so be ready with fenders and strong ropes securely fastened to bow, stern and mid-ships. If you can pass a strong rope right round the hull amidships, that will give a very strong securing point that could keep the boat afloat if it was tied to a larger vessel. As with every emergency, prevention is better than cure so check through-hull mountings, joins and exposed hatches, and repair or replace if you have any doubts at all.

## Grounding

Running aground can be either embarrassing or dangerous, depending where you do it and what you run on to. Most experienced sailors have run aground many times, and most groundings are the result of human error – missing a channel marker and sheer lack of attention are the two most common causes.

The type of hull and engine configuration will make it either easier or more difficult to get out of trouble. Having run aground, the first thing you need to do is get off and floating again, which might not be as easy as you would like. On outboard and out-drive powered boats, the first part of your boat to touch bottom is that highly vulnerable propeller, so as you ground your engine will probably stop as well. Do not try and re-start it until you are sure you have enough water under you again, and if you were heading into the shallows when you grounded, or wind is blowing you further onto shallow water, you will have to find some way of getting off before starting up.

By lifting the engine or leg, you will reduce the draft of the boat and you will be able to float clear, but do not do that unless you are sure the boat will drift clear rather that drift further into shallow water. Leave it down – at least it will hold you in place while you work out what to do. If you think you will drift off, raise the engine and help the boat along by poling with a boathook. While the engine is up, check the propeller. If it appears undamaged, lower the engine and try re-starting. Do not try and start the engine with the propeller raised – on an out-drive this will damage the transmission and on an outboard it may result in the water pump being damaged through dry-running.

If the engine races, you may have broken the cotter pin that holds the propeller in place. This is designed to break before the propeller is damaged, so provided you have a spare, the necessary tools and long arms you may be able to replace it. If the blades are bent, you will still be able to make progress but keep the speeds low as the vibration from unbalanced blades can damage bearings in the transmission.

If the wind is blowing you further onto the shallows, by raising the engine all you will do is allow the wind to push you into even shallower water. You will need to find some other means of getting off. If the tide is dropping, you will have to act quickly or you will be left high and dry until the tide rises again, which can be up to twelve hours later – or weeks later, if you ran aground on the top of a Spring tide!

A quick way of pulling a boat off is by pulling against an anchor. The best anchor to use is your lightest spare anchor, with only rope attached, not chain. You will be pulling at a low angle so chain is not needed. Stand somewhere on the boat with plenty of space, coil down some rope so it will run out freely, and throw the anchor as far as you can into deeper water. The best way of doing this is to stand on the bows, and swing the anchor like a giant pendulum to build up some momentum, then give it a mighty heave. Pull on the rope to bed the anchor, then raise your engine. This should leave the boat clear of the bottom and you can pull the boat out to deeper water. You may have to repeat this performance if you were not able to throw the anchor far enough to take you into deeper water.

If the tide is rising, you only need to wait a while and you will float free, but if the wind is blowing you onto the obstruction, carry out the anchoring throw as described above to hold the boat in position and prevent it from being driven onto the bank or rock as the tide rises.

If you are unlucky enough to ground on a bank in open water where there are waves, you need to get yourself off as quickly as possible to prevent serious structural damage caused by the wave action lifting the hull and dropping it onto the hard bottom. Plenty of vessels have grounded on exposed banks without serious damage, only to be pounded to destruction by wave action. The only action you can take is the same as described above, but if that proves difficult and your position is exposed, then you must alert the Coastguard as soon as possible because you will need the assistance of the rescue services.

Be wary of asking other vessels to come to your aid – if they draw as much water as your boat, they are in danger of ending up in the same situation as you are. Unless there is serious and imminent danger to life, it is better to wait for a more suitable craft with an experienced crew to come to your aid.

If you have grounded and managed to get yourself free, you need to inspect the underside of the boat before heading out to sea. If the incident happened on the way out, then you must resist the temptation to carry on because you may have damaged the engine, propeller, hull or fittings. Only when you are sure there is no risk of engine failure or leaks should you proceed out to sea.

## Getting Lost

It is very easy to jump in a boat and head out to sea, it is less easy to find your way back in again, or find your way into a different landing place, even with the help of modern, low cost electronic navigation aids. If you have not set navigational waypoints all the way back to your landing site but instead relied on memory and recognition to find your way back, you may be surprised how different the land looks from a different direction, with a different light angle and perhaps a different height of water.

The main reason for this is because land viewed from the sea appears as a solid unbroken line – you cannot easily discern headlands, bays, harbour estuaries and landmarks from a short distance out to sea, whereas from above, such as on a hill or cliff top, and particularly from a chart, these features are strikingly obvious.

If you are heading out from a launch ramp or harbour and are planning to return to the same point, first mark the launch point on your GPS with the "Mark" feature – this is more reliable and accurate than working it out from your chart. As you go out to sea, also mark additional waypoints in the same way, particularly if your route from the launch point to your fishing mark is not a straight line. As a minimum, mark a waypoint at a point in the sea where there is no danger areas such as rocks or headlands between that point and your fishing marks, and where you can easily find your way back to the launch site even in poor visibility. Keep looking around and back as you head out to sea, and try and remember the look of the land so you recognise it on your return journey.

If you are intending to travel to a different point of landing, do not rely just on a chart and a GPS to find your way. Refer to a book known as a "Pilot" which will describe safe approaches, local hazards and other useful information for areas you will be visiting. The Pilots are available from local yacht chandlers and are intended for cruising yachts, and cover either localised areas or much wider cruising grounds. These are good investments, as they are written by boat owners for boat owners and will contain all the useful and essential information you will need in order to find your way around unfamiliar areas safely.

If you genuinely become lost, do not motor around hoping you will find your way home. You will be in danger of running out of fuel, or hitting unexpected rocks or shoals. Call the Coastguard, they may be able to get at least one bearing on your radio transmission, or don't be embarrassed to call another boat and ask them.

## Fog

Fog, or other precipitation like torrential rain or snow, can limit visibility to a dangerous degree. You may know where you are, you may be able to track your course and steer entirely by GPS, but if you cannot see more than a few metres you can easily miss a narrow harbour entrance, or see another vessel too late to take sufficient avoiding action.

If the visibility is too poor for safe navigation, do not risk your boat and crew, it is better to delay your start than be run down by a large ship. However, poor visibility can come upon you unexpectedly, so you may have to find your way home.

If you know where you are and can navigate by GPS, then the only additional precaution you can take is to have a very good lookout posted outside the cabin – they will need to spot the faintest glimmer of boat and shore through the fog, and even a clean window will inhibit this. If the journey is lengthy, it is a very good idea to swap lookout duties around so concentration does not flag. Your safety is entirely dependant on the lookout spotting pot floats, floating obstructions, rocks and other vessels before you hit them.

Keep speeds low enough for the visibility, if the fog is very thick then it is better to get home at a crawl than go too fast to avoid something that suddenly appears out of the fog.

If you do not have GPS or are not confident of finding your way home, then as long as you are not in a dangerous position such as a shipping lane, it would be prudent to anchor and wait for conditions to improve. If you decide to wait, make sure someone on shore knows what you are doing so they do not worry about your non-arrival and alert rescue services.

## Night

If you plan to be out at night, then night travel does not need to be in this section. However, you may find yourself travelling at night as a result of delays from other causes, and if you are unfamiliar with navigating at night this can be a very unsettling experience.

In some ways, night navigation is easier – lighted buoys are recognisable from their flashes at a great distance, which is not possible in daylight. Other vessels are also highly visible, and it is easier to determine their direction of travel from their lights than it would be from a vague shape in daylight.

In other ways it is more tricky – you cannot see floating obstructions or pots, and the mass of lights in a busy shipping area can be bewildering for the novice night-time navigator. It is also difficult to see an unlit shore, so familiar landmarks cannot be used as a point of reference.

When under way at night, you must have the correct navigation lights. For low speed powered vessels under 7 metres in length a single white visible from all directions is all that is needed, so even if you do not intend to travel at night you should fit such a light just in case. The same light is used for vessels at anchor, so if you decide to sit the night out at anchor, the same light will serve you in good stead.

Tip:

Maintaining good night vision is essential, and the only way to do this is to keep all lights on board as low as possible. One glimpse at a bright light can reduce your night vision for up to thirty minutes. Internal lights are available with alternative red and white switches - at least one of these in the wheelhouse or cuddy switched to red will mean you can illuminate charts and instruments without blinding yourself when you look back out to sea.

You may not be able to judge the height of incoming waves, so you are more likely to be taken be surprise if you encounter a rogue wave or a ship's wake. If anyone goes over the side at night, it will be far more difficult to find and recover them, so if you can persuade your crew to use lifelines you can be more sure of their safety.

Remember you cannot easily see unlit obstructions, so keep the speed down and keep a good lookout. A well-prepared night passage can be quite a thrill, so being caught out at night need not be too bad if you make your way back carefully and take all reasonable precautions to stay safe.

# Basic Maintenance and DIY

There are many books on boat maintenance and repair, so this section will cover only the basics for anglers who may be new to boat ownership. Wooden boats require a great deal of dedication and skill to maintain, which is outside the scope of this book. In this section we will cover the basic day to day maintenance and simple repairs on GRP boats, engines and trailers.

## Cleaning Fibreglass Boats

A brand new fibreglass boat looks as though it will never become dirty. A few months and a few fishing trips later it might not look so pristine. New boats will have a smooth shiny gel coat, with probably a couple of coats of polish on top. Dirt can be easily hosed off with fresh water. You should hose your boat down with fresh water after every salt water trip, as salt crystals are sharp and can scratch the gel coat and polycarbonate windows. Salt is highly corrosive, and even stainless steel will rust eventually. It is best to flush salt from all parts of the boat to prevent damage.

As the original polish wears off and sunlight and abrasion start to work on the gel coat, the microscopic porosity of the gel coat surface traps dirty marks and is more difficult to keep clean. Surfaces with non-slip markings such as decks are particularly prone to marking. Any household detergent cleaning liquids can be used, and common household bleach is particularly good for grubby decks. Pour neat bleach on the deck, and give it a scrub to spread it out and work it in a bit. Leave it for fifteen minutes, give it another scrub and rinse off. A pressure washer is good for rinsing but you don't really need it, it just makes it quicker.

If marks still remain, you can remove them with fibreglass polishing compound. This is a very mild abrasive that actually cuts into the surface, so any stains embedded in the gel coat are removed. This also restores the shine to the gel coat, but does involve a lot of elbow grease. For large areas it is worth investing in an electric polisher with removable mop heads for cutting and polishing. Older boats will need an annual all-over polish to maintain their appearance and an electric polisher will be invaluable.

To maintain a good finish and minimise the staining from dirt, follow up the cutting polish with a top polish to seal the surface. If you can spare the time, two coats of polish will give an excellent surface protection.

Stainless rails need a rinse, and every now and again a polish with a metal polish will maintain the shine. Glass and polycarbonate windows need a good flush with water – don't wipe dried salt from a polycarbonate window as this may scratch it. To make it easier to see out of wet windows, you can apply a special window polish that coats the window surface, inside or out, with a chemical that repels water. Drops form into beads that quickly run off, preventing fogging on the inside and making it easier to see out of windows that are not cleared by a wiper blade.

# Antifouling

If you keep your boat afloat, the hull surface and parts of the engine that are permanently under water will soon attract weed growth, particularly near the surface where the penetration of sunlight is at its maximum. Weed growth is unsightly and will slow the boat down significantly. Heavy growth can even block cooling water inlets for the engine.

To prevent weed growth, you need to paint the underwater part of the hull with an antifouling paint, obtainable from yacht chandlers. This paint is expensive compared to normal yacht paint. There are several different types of antifouling, designed for different uses – slow sailing boats, fast racing yachts and power boats, fresh water, sea water and warm water. The manufacturers produce comprehensive guides to help you choose the right type of antifouling paint, and calculate how much you will need. If you are applying antifouling on GRP that has not been previously painted, it must be applied over a suitable primer.

Antifouling is an unpleasant substance that inhibits weed growth, and slowly leaches away under water providing a constant surface of fresh paint. After a season, the paint will need renewing and is usually done as part of an annual out-of-water refit.

Provided the paint is sound, all that is needed is a rub down with wet-and-dry paper used wet, then after a rinse with fresh water, the new antifouling can be applied over the old. If you are using the same antifouling for the new coat as you did for the old, there will be no problems. If you are planning to use a different type, check for compatibility as some types cannot be applied over others. If the two are not compatible, you will have to strip off the old coat, re-prime and paint as for new antifouling.

Standard paint brushes or small rollers can be used. Antifouling paint is thick and heavy, so a narrow roller is easier to manage. If you buy cheap rollers from a DIY store, you can afford to throw the roller away rather than clean it. Cheap brushes are not worth buying as they have a tendency to shed hairs which are very annoying to have to remove from wet paint. Masking tape can be used to help create a nice sharp line on the waterline.

Antifouling paint is nasty stuff, so wear protective clothing: eye protection, overalls, a breathing mask and gloves are essential. Take care not to create dust, and dispose of flaked paint and contaminated materials safely. A special thinners is required to clean brushes and rollers, so remember to buy some at the same time as buying the antifouling paint.

As the boat will be on a trailer or blocks when you apply the paint, there will be patches of hull under the blocks or props. Do not try and remove the props, this is highly dangerous and could cause the boat to topple. Instead, pour a small quantity of paint into a jam jar with a lid, and leave this and a small paintbrush with the yard staff who will be re-launching the boat. They can paint the patches when the boat is in slings ready to go back in – this is common practice in well-run boatyards.

If you have an out-drive leg, you can buy a special antifouling paint designed specifically for these surfaces. The original high gloss finish needs to be rubbed down to create a key for the paint, which may seem a pity – but nobody will notice. If you want to preserve decals or graphics, these can be masked with tape before painting. Be careful not to paint over grease nipples, electrical earth connections, hydraulic rams or sacrificial anodes.

## Electrolysis

Electrolysis is a confusing and misused term in the boating world. It is loosely applied to the corrosion processes, referring to the degradation of an electrolyte that occurs as a result of passing electrical current through it. The confusion in terms is usually between electrolytic corrosion and galvanic corrosion. Galvanic corrosion is caused by an electric current generated by two different metals in a conducting medium such as seawater. The results of each type of corrosion can be similar and can occur at an alarming rate.

Whenever different metals are placed in a conductive liquid you create a form of battery. If you connect these pieces of metal together, current will flow. The current will be removing metal from one of the metal pieces, which is the "electrolysis". If one of the pieces is a metal part of your boat or engine, it will be damaged.

To protect valuable metals parts, a block of zinc called a sacrificial anode is bolted to key metal components such as the out-drive leg. Zinc is used because it has a higher voltage in the water so the current will be more inclined to flow from it than from your out-drive leg. If you keep your boat in the water, it is essential that these anodes are replaced regularly (every year or two), as they corrode away. They must never be painted over, and the electrical contact between the anode and the metal parts they are intended to protect must be good. Parts commonly protected in this way are the out-drive leg, which may have several custom-shaped anodes; trim tabs, prop shaft and metal rudder.

# Fibreglass Repairs

Fibreglass boats can take quite a pounding before suffering serious damage, but even a minor bump or scrape can cause an unsightly scratch or chip. If the scratch does not go deep enough to expose the fibreglass matting, then it is only cosmetic damage. Deeper scrapes must be repaired to ensure that water does not creep into the matting and create wet spots in the hull.

Minor scratches can usually be polished out very easily. If they cannot be removed with rubbing compound, use a very fine wet and dry paper used wet – 1000 or 1200 grade – and finish with rubbing compound. This will cut into the gel coat so be careful not to sand too much away.

Deeper chips and scrapes can be repaired with a gel-coat repair kit available from good yacht chandlers. White is the most popular colour, but other pigments can be found if you have a coloured hull. This might sound odd but there are many colours of white so your repair might not be a perfect match, but it will be close enough for most people.

To repair a gel-coat chip, choose a dry, warm day and thoroughly clean the hole and surrounding area. Don't be afraid of gouging the area with a sharp knife – it is better to have a larger hole to fill that have unsightly dirt marks embedded in the repair. Mix a small quantity of gel-coat and hardener in a non-metallic pot. The ratios are usually easy to calculate by squeezing equal lengths of paste from the two tubes – the difference in the diameters of the tubes are calculated to give the correct ratio. If the day is cool, you can speed up the setting process by using slightly more hardener – you are more likely to need this if the repair site is very small, as the setting is achieved by a chemical reaction causing heat. A larger quantity has a smaller surface area to volume ratio so it will retain heat and set more readily.

Mix the paste very thoroughly and apply with a plastic spatula. If the hole is large or on a steeply sloping surface it may "slump" – if that happens you can stick some tape over the wet paste to hold it in place while it sets. Apply enough paste to bring the surface slightly proud of the surrounding surface so you can sand it back perfectly level. If this is difficult on a large repair, you may need to apply a second layer after the first has hardened. Try to keep the fill even and without swirls or air bubbles that might be exposed when you sand the surface back.

Allow the repair to harden – this will take between ten minutes and half an hour depending on the temperature and your mix ratio. It will reach full strength a few hours later, but it is easier to sand once it has hardened but not reached full strength. Carefully sand the surface down using progressively finer wet-and-dry paper used wet, and bring the final surface back to a shine with rubbing compound. Finish off with a couple of coats of polish – with care you can repair even the ugliest gashes to look like new.

More serious repairs are outside the scope of this section but well within the capabilities of most DIY-ers. Holes can be repaired, modifications made or even complete replacement sections can be created using resin and fibreglass matting available from specialist suppliers. These suppliers can also provide free instruction sheets, and specialist books are available covering fibreglass repair and boat manufacture.

## Osmosis and Other Water Damage

Osmosis is the term given to fibreglass hull damage caused by water getting into the fibreglass matting and causing the layers to bubble or separate. This weakens the hull and must be repaired. Severe osmosis can be seen as a bubbling effect on the hull, but early warning can be given by periodically checking the hull with a moisture meter. Dampness in the fibreglass will show up on the moisture meter, which indicates that water is in the hull and will potentially cause the matting to blister or separate.

The only cure for osmosis is to thoroughly dry the hull, which can involve leaving the hull in a shed with electric heaters for several weeks. The surface layers are cut off, and any blistered matting cut right back. The hull surface is then plastered back and sanded down. Having invested in this amount of work it is worth going a step further and applying several layers of epoxy. This will completely seal the hull and prevent further occurrences of osmosis.

External osmosis damage to the hull usually only occurs in boats kept afloat for long periods. The same effect can occur on boats kept ashore if they are not drained properly – only on the inside of the hull rather than the outside.

A more common problem for small boats kept ashore is damage caused by water getting into places where it is not meant to be, and soaking into internal structures. Most boats have reinforcing strips of wood or foam in the hull which are fibreglassed over during construction. The transom will also have a heavy slab of plywood built into its core. Some boats also have false floors, with the gap between the hull and floor filled with foam. If water gets into foam, wood or voids it is very difficult to remove. Wet wood tends to expand and this can split the fibreglass making the problem worse. The only cure is to cut the damage out completely, working from inside the boat, replace the wood and re-laminate fibreglass over the top. This is a major job, but mostly in terms of labour. If you are prepared to do this type of repair yourself it need not be too expensive, although it will be very messy.

Prevention is better than cure so make sure the open parts of the boat are covered by a tonneau cover or tarpaulin, and any water is free to drain quickly away. If you store your boat with drain plugs out, remember where you put them and make sure you replace them before launching.

All engines need regular servicing to ensure they are reliable and get you home safely. You should also carry out regular maintenance checks in between services to ensure they are kept in the best possible condition.

# Engines

## Outboard Engines:

- Store upright, not tilted, so water drains away and does not collect and corrode the vulnerable alloys.

- Wash the outside of the engine with fresh water after every sea trip.

- Flush the engine cooling system with fresh water. You can buy hose adaptors called mufflers which connect a garden hose to the water intake of the engine. Turn the water supply on before you start the engine, and run the engine gently for a minute or two to flush sea water out of the cooling system. Never run an engine without a water supply even for a few seconds – a water pump impeller depends on water for lubrication and will rip itself to shreds if it runs dry.

- Ensure the oil reservoir is kept topped up on two-stroke engines, and check the oil level on four-stroke engines before every trip.

- Check fuel lines for damage, and replace if they are perished or worn. The smallest hole can prevent the low pressure fuel pump from drawing sufficient fuel to run the engine.

- Visually check the engine for oil leaks and damage. Paint chips can be touched in with car paint. Damaged propellers can be repaired by specialists surprisingly easily. Make sure access panels and covers are secure and fitted correctly, as they are expensive to replace if they fall off at sea!

### Inboard:

- Allow the engine to idle for a few minutes before switching off – this allows it to cool down slowly.

- Check engine oil, hydraulic steering oil and if fitted, coolant levels and top up if necessary.

- Check visually for oil and coolant leaks.

- Check fuel trap bottles for contamination with dirt or water – drain off if necessary.

- Drain any water from the bilges under the engine, and sponge dry. Water can splash the starter motor and alternator when under way, quickly damaging them.

- Check battery connections for tightness, and ensure they have a covering of petroleum jelly to prevent corrosion.

- Check drive belt tensions and adjust if necessary.

- Leave the battery master switch and any sea-cocks set to the off position.

## Trailers

Trailers have a very hard life and are particularly vulnerable if they are dipped in sea water to launch the boat. After every launch and recovery, they must be rinsed thoroughly with fresh water, hosing into the brake drums and down any open tubes.

All grease points on the bearings, brake cables and hitch must be greased with a powerful grease gun using a waterproof grease designed for trailer bearings – any other type may not provide adequate protection or lubrication. Make sure Bowden cables are free to slide and are not sticking. If they require lubrication and are not provided with grease nipples, remove one end and temporarily fasten it to something solid facing upwards. Make a funnel around the open end with modelling clay, and pour oil down it until oil comes out of the other end. Make sure the oil does not get into the brake drums. This operation may take some time as the oil seeps through the cable.

It is worth spraying the hitch with WD-40, as this has the most exposed moving parts. Check visually for jammed or damaged rollers, and damage to the galvanised surface that could rust. Rollers need to be in good condition and free rolling to make launching and recovery easy and prevent risk of damage to the boat. It is better to replace a roller than have to repair the hull after a roller cracks and the hull is gouged.

If you have a winch, check the condition of the strap or wire. Any fraying could result in sudden breakage which could send your boat crashing down the slipway. Damaged straps and wire must be replaced. Also check the pawls and securing hooks, as a failure here could also give you serious problems in mid-launch.

Trailer tyres need looking after in the same way as your car tyres. Keep them pumped up to the correct pressure, and replace them if there is side wall damage or insufficient tread. Towing a trailer in an un-roadworthy condition is a motoring offence carrying heavy penalties, and an accident caused by a trailer failure at speed could be extremely serious.

# Adding and Replacing Fittings

If you are lucky enough to buy a new boat, it will be supplied with standard fittings already properly mounted in place. However, sooner or later you will want to fit additional items like rod holders, fender eyes, rails and so on. If your boat is second-hand, you may need to replace damaged items and add your own.

Adding fittings to boats is very straightforward for anyone with basic DIY ability, but it is not exactly the same as working on a car or a house. The marine environment is far more corrosive to fastenings and seawater can cause damage if not kept out, so additional care has to be taken. Fitting items to fibreglass, steel and wooden structures requires a similar approach.

If you are removing a fitting to replace it, you will find it has either been screwed directly to the fibreglass with a self-tapping screw, or bolted through the fibreglass with a washer and nut on the other side. After removing the fastenings and the fitting, you will probably find some encrusted white rubbery material underneath, which must be cleaned off. If the old holes are not in the correct place for your new fitting, the screw holes must be thoroughly cleaned out and filled with gel-coat repair paste before proceeding.

To add a new fitting, firstly think carefully about the location. You cannot fix directly to the skin of the hull, as drilling a hole through could cause a leak. You can add fittings to the hull if a wooden pad has been glassed into the hull, and this is common practice for the transom and strengthening ribs inside the hull. You can safely drill through gunwhales and internal mouldings as long as there is no danger of leaks.

The thickness of the fibreglass and the strength required for the fitting will determine whether you screw or bolt to the fibreglass. Mooring cleats, rail mountings and grab handles must always be through-bolted, preferably with an additional wooden or stainless steel pad sandwiched under the nuts on the other side to spread the load. If there is a thick wooden pad under the fibreglass, other fittings can be fixed with screws driven into the wood. If there is only thin fibreglass to fix to, short self-tapping screws can be used but do not use them on anything that is expected to take a load.

The type of screws to use is very important. Marine grade stainless steel must be used – even stainless steel used in external fittings in the construction industry are not of sufficient corrosion resistance to stand up to prolonged exposure to salt water. Brass screws can be used on wooden boats, but they are not tough enough to be driven into fibreglass.

When drilling holes for fixing screws to fibreglass, make the holes smaller than the external thread size, but larger than you would for normal wood screws. This is because fibreglass does not have the same "give" as wood, and if the screw is too tight you may not be able to screw it in, or worse, you could easily break it off in the hole if you apply too much turning force. However, as fibreglass is so much stronger than wood, you do not need such a deep grip of the screw threads to make a strong fastening. It is worth drilling the very top of the hole over-size to prevent the gel coat from chipping as the screw is run in.

When fitting any item to the external parts of a boat, you must prevent water seeping under the fitting and into the screw holes. This is particularly important on wooden boats, or if you are drilling into the internal woodwork of a fibreglass boat. When you fix the item to the boat, smear a layer of waterproof sealing compound under the item so it seals up the gap between the boat and the item you are fixing. There are several different types of sealant available from yacht chandlers, depending on the type of application. Silicone sealants are best avoided because they can come unstuck when they set, allowing water to seep in. They also fill the pores of the gel-coat making it impossible for any future sealant to fully bond to the surface. If you must use silicone, tighten up partially, allow the silicone to set, then tighten fully on the pad of silicone. Alternative sealants are more forgiving and the non-setting types give lasting protection.

## Boat Electrics

Your boat will probably have some basic electrical circuits already installed, with a battery, isolating switch, fuse panel and charging circuit. If not, then I recommend you read up on marine electrics before fitting any electrical items yourself. There are some very good books on the subject available from specialist bookshops and the larger yacht chandlers. This section covers the maintenance of your boat electrics, and the fitting of additional electrical items to an existing circuit. I am assuming your boat has a 12 volt system. There are 24 volt systems in common use but these are usually found on larger craft.

## Battery

Batteries have different characteristics depending on their intended use, and marine batteries are very different from car batteries. A boat battery will have long periods with no use, then deep loads as it is used to start a heavy engine. If you shop around, a marine battery need not cost significantly more than a car battery, and it will last considerably longer as it is designed for the use you are going to give it.

Marine batteries should give several years of trouble-free use provided they are cared for. Try and keep them fully charged, and if you are going to leave the boat for several months, it is better to remove the battery and keep it at home so you can give a top-up charge with a mains battery charger every three months. Marine batteries thrive on use, and one used and charged regularly will remain in good condition. Never leave a battery in a discharged state.

The only maintenance they need is an occasional check to ensure the liquid in the cells (electrolyte) is at the correct level, and if it is low, it needs to be topped up with distilled water. Make sure the battery is well secured, otherwise it will slide around with the motion of the boat which could strain the terminal posts, and banging can damage the internal plates. Battery terminal connectors need to be tight, but do not strain the post by excessive leverage with a spanner. When the connections are secure, wipe over the metal parts of the connections with ordinary petroleum jelly – this will prevent corrosion. A poor battery connection can give a very accurate impersonation of a flat battery, so if you think the battery should be fully charged but it fails to deliver the power you need, check the connections before charging up the battery again.

I prefer to have two batteries, particularly if I am planning to use electrics a lot during a trip – bait well aerators, lights, pumps, radio all add to the load and it would not be good to find they had drained your battery when you come to start again. You can fit two batteries in parallel, with an isolating switch so you can use one battery for "domestic" – a term given to the lights, pumps and other non-engine related electrics – and preserve the other battery for engine starting. You can charge both batteries from the engine while it is running. You must use a specialist marine battery switch however, to ensure the switch is adequate for the heavy loads. For more information on wiring up a dual battery set-up, refer to a marine electrics book on the subject. Some examples are provided in the Appendices.

## Adding Electrical Items

If you want to add additional electrical items such as lights or electronic navigation aids, you can mount the items as described the previous section on Adding and Replacing Fittings, and wire the electrics as follows.

Firstly, read the installation instructions if supplied, very carefully. This will usually give instructions on where to site the unit, and what power supply is required. You need to be careful where you route signal cables such as a VHF aerial cable or fish-finder transducer cable to avoid interference from other electrical currents. You will find that most electrical items will be mounted in or near the steering position or cuddy, and the battery is usually at the stern near the engine. If one is not already installed, you will need to fit a distribution panel at a central point near the instruments, and run a heavy duty positive and negative cable back to the battery to avoid having to run separate wires to the battery for each item.

The negative cable runs from the negative battery terminal to a metal bar called a "bus-bar" fitted usually behind the steering console, which has a number of contacts on it to which you can connect the negative wires from all the nearby electrical items. The positive cable runs from the battery isolating switch to a fuse panel mounted near the negative bus-bar. The fuse panel will have one connection for the heavy duty positive cable, which is linked to a number of fuses, and on the other side of each fuse will be a separate connection point for the positive cable from each electrical item you wish to connect. The fuse needs to be rated according to the specification in the instructions that are supplied with your electrical items.

Tips:

Keep a number of spare fuses in a plastic film canister or similar plastic pot with a lid, and attach the canister firmly to a position close to the fuse panel. If you have to change a fuse in a hurry, they will be close at hand.
Label the positive wires coming into the fuse panel so they are easily identified. Use a waterproof marker on a label that will not come off, or use wire marker sleeves you can purchase from electrical specialists.

The wires you use must be rated for the appropriate amperage for the required load on a 12 volt system. Household wiring must never be used. Auto cable can be used for boats usually kept ashore, but it is preferable, and essential for boats kept afloat, to use marine grade cable. This has an additional coating of tin over the copper wire to inhibit corrosion of the copper at the connection points.

To calculate the size of cable you need, use the simple formula

**Watts = Amps X Volts**

The easy way to remember is "WAVe" – even easier as you are working on a boat!

You know the voltage: it is 12. The wattage of the unit will be on the specification, so by inverting the formula you get

**Watts/Volts = Amps**

The fuse needs to be slightly higher than the calculated amperage, and you can afford to make the wire capable of handling a much higher load. If there is a long run of wire, the wire itself will case a resistance so it needs to be thicker to compensate. If you are in any doubt about what size of wire to use, ask for advice or refer to specialist books such as those listed in the Appendices.

Connectors must be marine grade connectors, and I prefer the crimp type with a spade end or eye depending on what it is to be connected to. Try and avoid connecting lengths of cable together, particularly where they may get wet. This can lead to corrosion and breakage. If you have to make a connection, use a crimp, and coat the crimp with a generous layer of silicone sealant. You can make a neat job of this by sliding a short length of larger tube over the wire before you make the connection, then slide it back and pump silicone sealant into the gap inside the outer tube. This will create an air and waterproof seal.

Take particular care where you route cables, particularly through the cockpit. It is a good idea to thread the two heavy duty cables through a length of plastic conduit of the type available from a DIY store, and fix the conduit under the cockpit floor or under the gunwhales. Keep your wires tidy with plenty of cable ties, or the spiral wrapping used to make wiring looms. The result not only looks very professional, it prevents tangles and protects the wires from being snagged and damaged by other things.

## Mounting a Fish-Finder Transducer

A fish-finder works by sending pulses through the water and measuring the time and strength of the return signal. The unit that sends these signals is the transducer, which must be mounted either in the water or on the inside face of a fibreglass hull, with no air space or bubbles between the face of the transducer and the water. The transducer must be mounted where the face of the transducer is on a horizontal plane, where no turbulence and bubbles in the water will pass in front of it. All of this will be described in detail in the fish-finder installation manual.

The position giving the best signal will be a transom mount, using the brackets supplied. If you chose to do this, make sure you use marine-grade screws, and a caulk sealant designed for underwater use. Route the cable up the transom to a point well above the waterline before drilling a hole and threading the cable through. The cable will have a connector for the unit already fitted, so you will have to drill a hole large enough to accommodate the connector. This will be larger than the hole required for the wire, so fill the gap with caulk sealant and cover the outside with a plate designed for the purpose – if one was not supplied with the fish-finder, they can be obtained from the larger yacht chandlers.

Alternatively, you can mount the transducer inside the hull, but only if you can find a suitable position. The transducer must be in a safe place where it will not be damaged by your fishing activities, where it can be mounted flat, and where it will shoot through solid fibreglass without the signal being obstructed by foam cores, wooden stringers or external turbulence. The mounting will require permanent fixing so you will need to test it before committing to a position, because if you fit it in the wrong place it will be very difficult to move. To create a trial mounting, make a "pond" of vegetable oil where you want to mount the transducer, using a quantity of modelling clay such as Plasticene for the walls of the pond, just large enough to accommodate the transducer. Place the transducer in the pond, and the oil will fill the gap between the transducer face and the hull, allowing the signal to pass through. Ask a willing crew member to hold it in place while you test the signal in the water, both at rest and under way, or if the crew proves unwilling or unreliable, make a sandbag by filling a strong plastic bag with damp sand and wedge the transducer in place with that.

One you have decided on the position for the transducer, clean away the Plasticene and oil, and thoroughly de-grease the inner hull surface and transducer face. There are two alternative means of fixing the transducer face to the inside of the hull – you can either use epoxy adhesive such as Araldite, or silicone sealant. In either case, use a generous quantity to make sure there are no gaps or air bubbles under the face of the transducer. If you are mixing adhesive, do it carefully so there are no air bubbles. Place a large blob of adhesive on the inner hull and press the transducer face down onto the blob, pushing down and making sure the transducer face is well seated in the adhesive. Wedge the transducer in place until it sets.

# Quick Test

Are you ready to go to sea, master of your own vessel? Try these questions to see how well you do. Making the wrong choice at sea would have more serious consequences.

1.  You are cruising along and suddenly notice a semi-submerged object right in front of you. It is too late to stop, do you turn to port or starboard?

2.  You see a patch of broken water in your course. What should you do?

3.  A power boat appears to be crossing your path from starboard to port. The angle at which it is approaching does not appear to change, so you are on a collision course. What should you do?

4.  A boat under sail appears to be crossing your path, this time from port to starboard. The angle at which it is approaching does not appear to change, so again you are on a collision course. What should you do?

5.  You are on a heading of 270° and this buoy is in front of you. Which side of it should you go?

6.  A power boat is coming up a narrow channel towards you. What should you do?

7.  You decide to anchor in a spot where the water is 20 metres deep. How much rope and chain should you let out to ensure the anchor holds securely?

8.  You are out at night and these lights are in front of you. What do you think it is?

9.  The inshore waters forecast issued by the Met Office gives visibility as "Poor". Is it safe to go to sea in this?

10. You see a large floating object near a busy channel, which might be a shipping container. Which VHF Channel should you use to call the Coastguard in a non-emergency situation such as this, to advise them?

11. You are heading home, into the setting sun. The channel markers are visible but you cannot determine the colours because of the light. Which side should you pass this one?

# Quiz Answers

1.  *You could turn either way, but if your boat has a single propeller, the turning circle will be tighter in one direction than another. It is better to know which way your own boat turns more responsively, and always turn in that direction to respond to an emergency.*

2.  *Broken water could indicate either a shoal or over-falls. If it is a shoal, you risk running aground. If you know it is over-falls, and the height of the waves are not a threat to your safety, you can proceed through them. If you are uncertain, alter course to avoid broken water and watch the depth on your fish-finder closely.*

3.  *You must alter course to starboard. Make an obvious alteration so the other vessel can see you have altered course.*

4.  *You must alter course to port, as a sailing vessel has right of way over a power vessel unless the vessel under power is constrained by depth. It is safer and more courteous to pass behind the sailing vessel.*

5.  *You are heading west and this is the Cardinal Buoy marking the south point of a submerged object such as a wreck, rock or shallows. You should alter course to port and leave the buoy to starboard.*

6.  *Both you and the other vessel must alter course if necessary to pass to starboard, leaving the other vessel on the port side of your own vessel.*

7.  *You will need between 3 and 5 times the depth of water, so pay out at least 60 metres and up to 100 metres of anchor rope.*

8.  *This is a very large vessel heading towards you and on your port side. If you alter course to starboard you will safely avoid it.*

9.  *"Poor" visibility is between 1,000 metres and two nautical miles, so this is perfectly safe for collision prevention. You may not be able to see land however, so make sure you have adequate navigational skills.*

10. *Always call Coastguard on Channel 16. They will probably ask you to go to Channel 67 and stand by, but do not call them initially on Channel 67.*

11. *This is the starboard channel marker, because the object on top of the post is triangular. Leave it on your starboard side and pass to port.*

# The End

To quote Winston Churchill:

*"This is not the end.*
*It is not even the beginning of the end.*
*But it is the end of the beginning."*

I hope this book has been useful. Without writing a whole book on each chapter, I cannot possibly cover all there is to know on each of the subjects. However, I have tried to provide enough information to help you get started safely, and you will be able to learn more from books, magazines, web sites, people you meet and your own experiences on the water. So hopefully this is not the end of a short book on boats, it is the end of the start of many years of enjoyable boating for you.

If you would like to comment on any aspect of this book, ask questions or just share your own experiences, I would be delighted to hear from you. Just send me an email addressed to:

**neville@boat-angling.co.uk**

I'm always keen to learn more about boats, fishing and the sea.

# Appendices

The following sections contain additional information:

- Useful Resources
- Beaufort Wind Scale
- Marine Terminology
- Speed and Distance Conversion

## Distress Cards

Copy the following cards in colour and have them laminated in your local print services shop. Keep them on board, preferably stuck somewhere very obvious – it might not be you that has to make the emergency call. **SOLAS V** requires all vessels to have this information on board.

## Boat Inventory

Copy the following page and use it to record details of your boat and equipment. This will be invaluable in the event of an insurance claim or theft.

N = Purchased new
S = Purchased second-hand

## Boat Maintenance Log

Copy the following page and use it to record details of work carried out on your boat.

## Other Templates

Copy the following sheets and use to build up your own reference file – **Fishing Log** and **Marks**.

# Useful Resources

These were correct at time of publication. Site addresses may have changed since then – if you find a "Page Not Found" message, go to the relevant Home Page on the URL provided, or do a Google search.

## Web Sites

| Subject | Description | Web Site |
|---|---|---|
| Charts | The UK Hydrographic Office, publishers of Admiralty charts | www.ukho.gov.uk |
| SOLAS V | Text of the safety regulations applying to pleasure boat users | www.mcga.gov.uk/publications/SITE |
| Met Office | Weather forecasts, and weather reference | www.metoffice.co.uk |
| Maritime Safety | A site where you can report dangerous incidents in confidence | www.chirp.co.uk |
| Wrecks | A comprehensive wreck site for divers and historians | http://users.pandora.be/tree/wreck/wrecksite/wrecksite.html |
| Tides | Free tide tables | www.ukho.gov.uk/easytide |
| Sea Angling | Angling Forums | www.anglersnet.co.uk www.worldseafishing.com |
| Sea Fishing News | UK news and catch reports updated monthly | www.harvey-mayson.co.uk/seaangling |
| Slipways | Comprehensive guide to boat launching locations | www.boatlaunch.co.uk |
| Boat Jumbles | Boat jumble sales by date and location throughout the UK | www.boatjumbleassociation.co.uk |
| RYA | Site containing general boating news, advice, courses and qualifications | www.rya.org.uk |
| HM Coastguard | Marine safety information | www.mcga.gov.uk |
| Lifeboats | News and sea safety guides | www.rnli.org.uk |
| Boats for Sale | Boats, engines and bits for sale | www.boatsandoutboards.co.uk |
| Commercial fishing boats and equipment | Database of second hand boats and equipment, and many useful links | www.findafishingboat.co.uk |
| Sea Fisheries Committees | There are different SFC for each area of the coastline around the UK. Not all have web sites. Those that do publish local by-laws and minimum fish sizes | Sussex: www.sussex-sfc.gov.uk North Eastern: www.neseafish.gov.uk Eastern: www.esfjc.co.uk North Western and North Wales: www.nwnwsfc.org South Wales: www.swsfc.org.uk Northumberland: www.nsfc.co.uk |

| Subject | Description | Web Site |
| --- | --- | --- |
| Fisheries Regulations | Marine Fisheries Agency | www.mfa.gov.uk |
| Promoting Fish | Information and recipes | www.seafish.co.uk |
| Fish Information | Global fish information resource | www.fishbase.org |

## Books

There is a vast selection of books available, most of them excellent, although some are written for the more experienced boat owner. Here is just a small selection of books that will expand on the subjects covered in this book.

*Powerboat Handbook*  Paul Glatzel
*Understanding the Rule of the Road*  Paul Boissier
*First Aid*  Collins Gem
*Simple GPS Navigation*  Mik Chinery
*Admiralty Tidal Stream Atlas (various editions and regions)*
    Admiralty Charts and Publications
*Boat Safety Handbook*  RYA Publications
*Knot Know-how*  Steve Judkins and Tim Davison
*VHF Radio*  RYA Publications
*The 12 Volt Bible*  Miner Brotherton (revised by Ed Sherman)
*Weather at Sea*  David Houghton
*Where to Launch Around the Coast*  Diana van der Klught
*Outboard Troubleshooter*  Peter White
*Marine Diesel Engines*  Nigel Calder
*Boat-owners Mechanical and Electrical Manual*  Nigel Calder
*Electrics Afloat*  Alastair Garrod

## Magazines

There is a good choice of magazines for a wide range of water sports, and it is noticeable that there is more choice in newsagents nearer the coast or larger navigable rivers. Monthly magazines of interest to owners of angling boats include:

- *Motor Boat Monthly*
- *Motor Boat and Yachting* (mainly larger cruising boats)
- *Practical Boat Owner* (mainly for sailing boats but has useful DIY features)
- *Boat Mart*
- *Buy a Boat for under £20,000*
- *Boats and Planes For Sale*

# Beaufort Wind Scale

**Francis Beaufort** was born in 1774 in County Meath, Ireland and began his nautical career at 13 as a cabin boy in the Navy. By the age of 22 Beaufort had risen to the position of lieutenant. Whilst on a patrol in 1812, he was injured in action. Unable to continue in active service he was given the position of Hydrographer to the Admiralty, and worked in the Navy until two years before his death in 1857, serving for 68 years.

Beaufort invented the **Beaufort Scale** in 1806 for his own use, and the Royal Navy adopted his method in 1838. Although over the next hundred years the Beaufort Scale was slightly modified, it is still based around Francis Beaufort's original concept. Many maritime weather forecasts refer to Beaufort wind speeds, although land-based forecasts usually describe wind speeds in knots or miles/kilometres per hour. Neither are particularly useful unless you know what the effect is, so the Beaufort Wind Scale is a useful visual reference for wind speeds and its likely effect on the water you want to fish in.

| Beaufort Force | Windspeed Knots | Description | Sea Condition |
|---|---|---|---|
| 0 | 0 | **Calm** | Sea like a mirror. |
| 1 | 1 – 3 | **Light Air** | Ripples but without foam crests. |
| 2 | 4 – 6 | **Light Breeze** | Small wavelets. Crests do not break. |
| 3 | 7 – 10 | **Gentle Breeze** | Large wavelets. Perhaps scattered white horses. |
| 4 | 11 – 16 | **Moderate Breeze** | Small waves. Fairly frequent white horses. |
| 5 | 17 – 21 | **Fresh Breeze** | Moderate waves, many white horses. |
| 6 | 22 – 27 | **Strong Breeze** | Large waves begin to form; white foam crests, probably spray. |
| 7 | 28 – 33 | **Near Gale** | Sea heaps up and white foam blown in streaks along the direction of the wind. |
| 8 | 34 – 40 | **Gale** | Moderately high waves, crests begin to break into spindrift. |
| 9 | 41 – 47 | **Strong Gale** | High waves. Dense foam along the direction of the wind. Crests of waves begin to roll over. Spray may affect visibility. |
| 10 | 48 – 55 | **Storm** | Very high waves with long overhanging crests. The surface of the sea takes a white appearance The tumbling of the sea becomes heavy and shock like. Visibility affected. |
| 11 | 56 – 63 | **Violent Storm** | Exceptionally high waves. The sea is completely covered with long white patches of foam lying in the direction of the wind. Visibility affected. |
| 12 | 64 + | **Hurricane** | The air is filled with foam and spray. Sea completely white with driving spray. Visibility very seriously affected. |

# Marine Terminology

**Abeam**  Alongside and usually parallel to the boat.

**Aft**  At the back (of the boat).

**Air draft**  Distance between the waterline and the highest part of the boat.

**Antifouling**  Paint used to prevent weed and animal growth on the underwater area of a boat kept afloat.

**Beach**  (verb) Drive a boat onto a shelving beach from the sea.

**Beam**  Width of a boat – or –"On the Port/Starboard beam" means at 90 degrees to the direction of travel on the left or right hand side.

**Bilges**  Inside bottom of the boat, usually the under-floor area.

**Bitt**  Small post, often with a horizontal bar running through it, on a boat or on shore, to which mooring ropes are secured.

**Boom**  Wooden or metal bar to hold the bottom of a sail.

**Broach**  Turn over or take a wave over the side as a result of the boat being at right angles to a large wave.

**Buoy**  Floating marker or floating mooring point.

**Bow(s)**  The front of the boat.

**Cable**  Anchor rope or anchor chain.

**Cable**  A historical unit of measure – 100 fathoms or 200 yards.

**Can**  Slang for buoy (often used in racing).

**Cill**  Some marinas have a gate which swings up to dam the water in the marina when the tide drops. This gate is called a cill.

**Coaming**  Upper edge or rim of the cockpit, usually of a sailing vessel.

**Courtesy Flag**  National maritime flag of the country you are visiting, flown from the crosstrees of a mast.

**Crosstrees**  The short horizontal projections part way up a mast.

**Dhan Buoy**  Small marker buoy with a mast for greater visibility.

**Dolphin**  Concrete, steel, wood or stone structure like a mini tower, used as a navigation marker.

**Draft**  Distance between the waterline and the lowest point of the keel.

**Dry-Berthing**  A marina berth where the boat is kept ashore and put in the water when the boat is required for use.

**Ensign**  National maritime flag, which may be different from the national flag. Flown at the stern to indicate nationality.

**Fairlead**  Rope guides, usually on the edge of the deck.

**Fiddles**  Ridges or rails around the edge or across tables and worktops to prevent objects sliding off.

**Force (wind)**  Wind speed according to the Beaufort Scale.

**Gunwhales** Pronounced "gunnals", the upper edge of the hull or side walls of the deck.

**Halliard** Rope used to raise a sail or a flag.

**Heel over** To tilt sideways at an angle, caused by wind, wave action or a heavy weight on one side of the boat.

**Helm** Steering position or to steer.

**Holding pontoon** A pontoon with limited waiting time, such as a pontoon to tie up against when waiting to enter a marina.

**Kedge** A secondary anchor.

**Keel** The lowest part of the underside of the boat.

**Keel-band** A metal band screwed to the bottom of the keel to protect it from scrapes.

**Lazarette** Engine bay or similar large under-floor area on larger boats.

**Leading marks** Posts, signs or symbols used to guide ships along safe channels by visually aligning two or more marks.

**Lee (in the/under the)** The position where you are sheltered from the wind such as by a headland, or a larger boat.

**Lee (shore)** Conversely, this is the shore that wind is blowing onto.

**Locker** Cupboard or fitted box with a lid.

**Log** Instrument to show the distance the boat has travelled or its speed.

**Mayday** Distress call.

**Moor** Tie a boat up alongside.

**Navigable** Where a boat may progress without danger of grounding.

**Painter** Mooring rope of a dinghy.

**Phonetic Alphabet** The alphabet using words for clarity rather than letters A – Alpha, B – Bravo etc.

**Piles** Posts, often arranged in pairs so boats can tie up to them from the bows and the stern. Used mainly in narrow estuaries and harbours. Also used as navigation markers, although they are usually then called posts!

**Pintles** Hinge part of a rudder, which is a metal peg attached to the stern of the boat.

**Port** The left hand side of the boat or on the left hand side of the boat (red). This was once called "larboard".

**Rowlocks** (pronounced "rollocks") The fork shaped devices. used to hold oars in position on the gunwhales.

**Running rigging** Ropes used to raise and control sails and spars.

**Sea-cock** A tap or valve controlling water coming into or going out of the boat through the hull, such as for a toilet or bait-well.

**Sea Room** Unobstructed space around a boat to allow it to complete the desired manoeuvre.

**Shackle**  D shaped screw connector, such as to attach an anchor to chain and chain to the eye of a rope.

**Sheets**  Ropes used to control a sail.

**Spar**  Wooden bars used to hold the top of a sail.

**Splice**  Method of joining ropes or making loops by weaving the strands of the end of a rope into the body of the rope.

**Standing rigging**  Ropes (usually wire) used to support a mast.

**Starboard**  The right hand side of the boat or on the right hand side of the boat (green).

**Steerage**  The ability to control the boat with the wheel. If the boat is going too slowly the wheel has no effect, so you have "no steerage".

**Stern**  The back end of the boat.

**Stern-gland**  A screw device to force grease into the bearings of a propeller shaft.

**Swinging Mooring**  A permanent mooring where the boat ties up to a buoy by the bows, and swings around it as the tide ebbs and flows.

**Warp (noun)**  A rope, usually a mooring rope.

**Warp (verb)**  To pull a boat along with a rope using the boat's own winches.

**Way (way on)**  Movement, or momentum.

**Weather (shore)**  The shore that wind is blowing away from.

# Speed and Distance Conversion

## Speed

| | | |
|---|---|---|
| 1 knot | = 1.15 mph | = 1.85 kph |

## Distance

| | | |
|---|---|---|
| 1 yard | = 3 feet | = .9144 metres |
| 1 fathom | = 6 feet | = 1.828 metres |
| 1 cable | = 200 yards | = 182.88 metres |
| 1 nautical mile | = 2,025.4 yards | = 1.852 kilometres |
| 1 nautical mile | = 1 minute of latitude | |

# Recognised Distress Signals

Red Parachute Flares

Orange Smoke

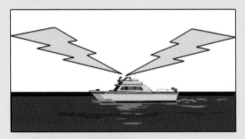

MAYDAY by radio

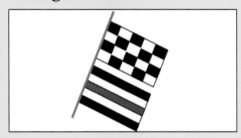

International Code Flag NC

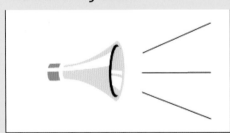

Continuous sounding of horn

Smoke and flames

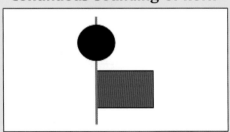

A square flag with a ball

Red Flare

SOS Morse code by lamp

Arms raised and lowered repeatedly

# DISTRESS CALL on CH 16

**Boat Name**

**Call Sign**

**Switch your VHF to Channel 16 at High Power, with dual-watch/Scan off, and check no-one is transmitting. Press the transmit button; say slowly and clearly:**

- **MAYDAY  MAYDAY  MAYDAY**
- **This is** ................................. boat name, repeat three times
- **MAYDAY, this is** .................... boat name, once
- **My position is** ......................... latitude and longitude; or give true bearing and distance from a known point. Repeat position if time allows
- **State nature of distress and type of assistance required:** vessel or person in grave danger e.g. sinking, fire, man overboard etc.
- **State number of people on board** ................................................. **OVER**.

  A MAYDAY signal imposes a general radio silence for all other vessels, and should be cancelled immediately the situation permits.

| | |
|---|---|
| **A** lfa | **N** ovember |
| **B** ravo | **O** scar |
| **C** harlie | **P** apa |
| **D** elta | **Q** uebec |
| **E** cho | **R** omeo |
| **F** oxtrot | **S** ierra |
| **G** olf | **T** ango |
| **H** otel | **U** niform |
| **I** ndia | **V** ictor |
| **J** uliet | **W** hiskey |
| **K** ilo | **X** -ray |
| **L** ima | **Y** ankee |
| **M** ike | **Z** ulu |

**Boat Inventory**

| Item | Make | Model | Serial No. | Date Purchased | N/S | Price Paid |
|---|---|---|---|---|---|---|
| Hull | | | | | | |
| Engine | | | | | | |
| Engine 2 | | | | | | |
| Trailer | | | | | | |
| GPS | | | | | | |
| Chart-plotter | | | | | | |
| Fish-finder | | | | | | |
| Fixed VHF | | | | | | |
| Handheld VHF | | | | | | |
| | | | | | | |
| | | | | | | |
| | | | | | | |
| | | | | | | |
| | | | | | | |
| | | | | | | |
| | | | | | | |
| | | | | | | |
| | | | | | | |
| | | | | | | |

**Boat Maintenance Log**

| Date | Work Done | Parts Fitted | Cost |
|------|-----------|--------------|------|
|  |  |  |  |

**Fishing Log**

| Date | Weather | Tide & Sea Conditions | Marks | Catch | | | Bait/Method |
|------|---------|----------------------|-------|-------|--|--|-------------|
| | | | | Species | No./weight | | |
| | | | | | | | |
| | | | | | | | |
| | | | | | | | |
| | | | | | | | |
| | | | | | | | |
| | | | | | | | |
| | | | | | | | |
| | | | | | | | |
| | | | | | | | |
| | | | | | | | |
| | | | | | | | |
| | | | | | | | |
| | | | | | | | |
| | | | | | | | |
| | | | | | | | |
| | | | | | | | |
| | | | | | | | |
| | | | | | | | |
| | | | | | | | |

**Marks**

| Name/Number | Description | Latitude | Longitude | Comment |
|---|---|---|---|---|
|  |  |  |  |  |
|  |  |  |  |  |
|  |  |  |  |  |
|  |  |  |  |  |
|  |  |  |  |  |
|  |  |  |  |  |
|  |  |  |  |  |
|  |  |  |  |  |
|  |  |  |  |  |
|  |  |  |  |  |
|  |  |  |  |  |
|  |  |  |  |  |
|  |  |  |  |  |
|  |  |  |  |  |
|  |  |  |  |  |
|  |  |  |  |  |
|  |  |  |  |  |
|  |  |  |  |  |
|  |  |  |  |  |
|  |  |  |  |  |
|  |  |  |  |  |

**Neville Merritt** was brought up near the Blackwater estuary, and was boating before he could walk. After a near-disaster in a storm the family sailing exploits were curtailed, but he took up fishing very soon after. Neville caught his first fish using a Woolworths rod, and boats and fishing have been his passion ever since.

When he was a teenager, his father bought a Norwegian fishing boat in which they both learnt a great deal about boats and the sea. Neville bought his own boat as soon as he could afford one, and has owned boats ever since.

He lives in Hampshire with his very understanding family, and fishes from his boat whenever he can off the Hampshire and Sussex coasts. Neville is also a keen fly and coarse fisherman.